WALK

C000070835

WEST OF IRELAND

THIRD EDITION

Tony Whilde & Patrick Simms

GENERAL EDITOR
JOSS LYNAM

Gill & Macmillan

Gill & Macmillan Ltd
Goldenbridge
Dublin 8
with associated companies throughout the world
www.gillmacmillan.ie

Maps drawn by Justin May
0 7171 2634 X

Print origination by
Seton Music Graphics Ltd, Bantry, Co. Cork and
Typeform Repro Ltd, Dublin
Printed in Malaysia

3 5 7 6 4

Tony Whilde, co-author of this guidebook, died
from a brain tumour on 8 February 1995. Ecologist,
walker, author and lecturer, he devoted much of his
life and career to the conservation of the West of
Ireland, which he loved. His untimely death is a
tragedy for all who knew him and shared his
affection for the West.

CONTENTS

MOUNTAIN SAFETY

The Irish hills are still relatively unfrequented. This is a happy situation for hill walkers unless they get into serious trouble and need help. As this may well have to come from a considerable distance, it is particularly important to take all reasonable precautions.

1. Wear suitable clothing, and regardless of the weather carry extra warm clothes, wind- and water-proof anorak and overtrousers. Except on short, easy walks it is best to wear walking boots.

2. Plan your walk carefully and be sure you can complete it before dark. To estimate walking times see page 3.

3. Check weather forecasts and keep a look out for weather changes. On high ground mist and rain can close in with alarming speed.

4. Remember that the temperature drops 2-3° for each 300m/1,000ft you climb and if, as is frequently the case, there is a strong wind the temperature drop will be even more marked. It may be a pleasant day at sea level whilst freezing and windy at 800m/2,500ft.

5. Always carry a map and compass, and learn to use them efficiently in good weather so you will have confidence in your ability to use them in bad. A torch, whistle and small first aid kit should also be taken — remember that the mountain distress signal is six blasts per minute and then a pause.

6. Carry a reserve supply of food including chocolate, glucose tablets, etc., and something warm to drink.

7. Leave word at your hotel, guest house or hostel where you are going, what your route will be and when you intend to get back. If you are parking a car at the beginning of a walk, you can leave a note on the seat.

8. Streams in flood are dangerous and extreme caution is necessary.

9. If your party does have an accident, telephone 999 and ask for the Mountain Rescue or contact the local Garda Station who will organise the rescue.

10. Never walk solo, except in areas where there are other people around.

11. Remember that most accidents happen on the descent, when you are tired, so take especial care then.

Some of the precautions listed above are obviously designed for the longer, higher walks but do remember that especially in winter, the Irish hills can be dangerous.

PROTECTING THE COUNTRYSIDE

Ireland has recently introduced a new Occupiers' Liability Act — dealing with the liability of farmers or other landowner for accidents which may happen to a walker or other user crossing their land. The act creates a new category of 'Recreational Users' who, when they enter farmland, are responsible for their own safety and for the safety of any children in their care. This will, it is to be hoped, make farmers, who have been worried about the possibility of claims following accidents to walkers, more willing to permit walkers to cross their land. The Irish Farmers Association, working with the Mountaineering Council of Ireland and other user bodies, has drawn up the following code to which all walkers and other users should adhere:

The Farmland Code of Conduct

* Respect farmland and the rural environment.
* Do not interfere with livestock, crops, machinery or any other property which does not belong to you.
* Guard against all risks of fire.
* Leave all farm gates as you find them.
* Always keep children under close control and supervision.
* Avoid entering farmland containing livestock. Your presence can cause stress to livestock and even endanger your own safety.
* Do not enter farmland if you have dogs with you, even on a leash, unless with the permission of the occupier.
* Always use gates, stiles or other recognised entry points.
* Take all litter home.
* Do not pollute water supplies.
* Take special care on country roads.
* Avoid making unnecessary noise.
* Protect wildlife, plants and trees.
* Take heed of warning signs — they are there for your protection.
* If following a recognised walking route, keep to the way-marked trail.
* Report any damage caused by your actions to the farmer or landowner immediately.
* Do not block farm entrances when parking.

MAPS AND SCALES

The Republic of Ireland is in the process of a complete re-survey and re-issue of its small scale maps, changing from imperial to metric units. Fortunately for the user all the walks in this guidebook can be found on the new 1:50,000 maps. While the new maps are a great improvement on the old 'half-inch' (1:126,720) maps, they are prepared from air surveys and are not entirely dependable in the marking of tracks and paths. The re-survey has inevitably involved some revision to heights. These revisions have not been transferred to the text or the sketch maps, but the reader should have no difficulty in equating spot heights. Mostly, the changes are of the order of 1–3m, but occasionally (as in Walk 48, Lavagh Beg has grown 40m!) the changes are substantial.

The sketch maps in this book will give you a good idea of your route, but they are hardly sufficient, especially on the more mountainous walks, as complete guides, and you are strongly advised to use the relevant topographical map.

Where heights or distances are approximate, as in 'walk 300yds along the road and turn off at a stile', we have not been pedantic and converted this to '274.3m' but, since the instruction is clearly to give an approximate distance, have simply written '270m/300yds'.

We recommend the following maps:

Ordnance Survey Maps
1:250,000 Holiday Maps Sheets 1 (North) and 2 (West) (These are suitable for general planning.)
1:50,000 Discovery Series (Republic of Ireland OS) and **Discoverer Series** (Northern Ireland OSNI). The relevant sheets are noted below each sketch map.

Other Useful Maps
Folding Landscapes, Roundstone, publish the following:
* *Mountains of Connemara*, a guidebook which has 1:50,000 maps covering the Twelve Bens and Maumturk Mountains. It has the advantage that it shows many walks complete, which, because of unfortunate sheet lines, require two or even three OS sheets.
* Connemara (1 inch to 1 mile).
* Burren (1:35,000).

Walking Times: Walking times have been calculated on the basis of 4km per hour, and 400m ascent per hour. This is roughly equivalent to 2½ miles per hour, and 1,300ft ascent per hour. These are fairly generous, and should allow you the occasional stop to admire the view, look at the map, take photographs, or recover your breath. They do not allow for protracted lunch stops! Extra time has been allowed if the going is difficult, and vice versa.

3

CLIMATE AND WEATHER

The climate and weather of the west of Ireland have a profound influence on human activities, including hill walking, and those venturing into the hills should have some knowledge and understanding of the conditions they are likely to meet.

The climate of western Ireland is largely the product of a westerly atmospheric circulation, and its proximity to the Atlantic Ocean. These two factors interact to give us westerly winds, mild damp weather and a narrow temperature range throughout the year.

Although the weather is highly variable there are a number of climatic features which appear to occur fairly regularly. During December and January there is a well-established low pressure system over the Atlantic spawning depressions which move rapidly eastwards, bringing strong winds and abundant frontal rain. By late January the cold anti-cyclonic weather centred over Europe may be extending westwards into Ireland giving dry, cold spells, eminently suitable for hill walking. From February to June the cold European anti-cyclones, reinforced sometimes by a south-ward extension of the Greenland anti-cyclone, tend to produce the driest period of the year. Towards late June or early July pressure rises over the ocean and falls over the continent, initiating a westerly, water-laden air-flow over Ireland. Cloud cover, humidity and rainfall increase and thunder becomes more prevalent, particularly during the warmer periods of August. Cold northerly air may bring active depressions in late August and September, but these can be interrupted by spells of anti-cyclonic weather. In October and November rain-laden westerlies predominate, although an incursion of anti-cyclonic conditions can bring good daytime weather.

Prevailing winds are south-westerly and westerly but as noted earlier, winds from the north and east may occur in anti-cyclonic conditions. The winds are lightest from June to September, and strongest from November to March, with January producing some of the severest gales.

May tends to be the sunniest month with an average of 6–7 hours of bright sunshine per day. Surprisingly, however, July tends to be relatively dull, with less bright sunshine then either June or August.

Snow is fairly uncommon in our mild maritime climate, occurring in brief spells usually in January and February, although it does occur on the high tops and in sheltered north-facing corries from November to April, and occasionally into May.

Looking more closely at Connemara, we find that the mountains receive, on average, 2,000 to 3,000mm (80 to 120 inches) of rain per annum, mainly in autumn and winter. The lower hills of Mayo, south Galway and Clare receive 1,200 to 2,000mm (48 to 80 inches) annually. Inland the rain is about half that recorded in the mountains and on the coast. To appreciate the way the mountains 'attract' rain, it is instructive to stand on Tawin Point (the peninsula which divides inner Galway Bay) in bright sunshine and watch the rain clouds roll over the Burren and Connemara. Finally, if it is not already apparent that waterproofs are an essential item of equipment in the hills, there are on average 225 'wet days' in Connemara and the mountains of Mayo and 200 in the Burren annually, that is days on which more than 1mm of rain falls. However, the scene is not really as dismal as these figures suggest because rarely does it rain continuously for more than a few hours, and most climbing days are blessed with dry periods.

Looking specifically at the northwest, we find that it is marginally cooler than southwest Ireland, the mean annual temperature at Malin Head in the period 1931–60 being 9.5°C. Rainfall in the mountainous districts averages 2,000mm to 2,500mm (80 to 100 inches) annually, with the wettest place recorded at Brockahy in the Blue Stacks, with an annual average of 2,719mm (109 inches) in the period 1941–70. The lowlands receive on average 1,250 to 1,600mm (50 to 64 inches) annually. There are on average 200 'wet days' annually over most of west Donegal and the Sligo and Ox Mountains, that is, days on which more that 1mm of rain falls. Mountains always attract clouds, as can be seen from any part of the northwest coast. One can observe the rain clouds passing overhead as for example on the Dawros peninsula to engulf higher ground inland around the Blue Stacks. Except during the rare heat-wave, water-proofs are an essential part of the walker's equipment. The rain, however, rarely falls for more than a few hours each day, so that the figures quoted above are not as dismal in reality. One can usually ignore that popular Irish saying: when you see the hills it's going to rain, and when you cannot it's raining already.

INTRODUCTION

Revising and updating a guide like this naturally invites comparison between 'then (1978) and now'. On the positive side, the hill tops and ridges are just as open and airy as before and still sufficiently remote from the noisy and changing world below to retain the magic I experienced in the early 1970s.

On the low ground, however, there are many physical and psychological shocks. Grant-aided barbed wire fencing now confines people as well as livestock, coniferous plantations make access to the hills difficult in places and houses have been built where tracks used to be. Progress for some is the limitation of freedom for others. As I write, pressure is mounting for the imposition of an airport beneath the 'Bens at Clifden. Extensive mining threatens several of our remotest valleys and some tourism developments bode ill for the tranquillity of the region.

As hill walkers we have to recognise the rights and aspirations of those who live and work in the countryside where we seek solitude and recreation. But, as we walk into the 1990s, it is becoming clear that the rights and aspirations of those who are attempting to impose long-term and devastating changes on the west of Ireland landscape must be tempered by the concerns, sensitivity and love we have for the countryside.

Since I wrote the first edition of this guide many people, I'm pleased to say, have *taken* great pleasure from walking in the hills of Clare, Connemara and Mayo. But times have changed and part of the pleasure for walkers in the future must come from *giving*. Giving of time, spirit and effort to keep the hills accessible, clean, quiet and healthy.

I would like to acknowledge the useful comments and help I have received from Dr David Harper (geology), Tim Robinson (place names), Clare and Gordon Young and Liz Kennedy. Joss Lynam kept me on my toes in his own, inimitable, but much appreciated manner. Marianne ten Cate typed the manuscript and to her I owe my special thanks.

Access and Accommodation

Access to the Burren and to the mountains of Connemara is relatively easy, but approaches to some of the Mayo mountains are more difficult.

One can travel from Dublin to Galway and Westport by main road or mainline rail. From Cork the bus route is more direct for those without a private means of transport. There are also flights from Britain and Dublin to Galway and Knock Airports.

Buses travel from Galway to the Burren via Kilcolgan, Kinvarra, Black Head, Ballynalackan and, finally, Lisdoonvarna, giving the walker ample opportunity to approach the hills from the north, west and southwest.

Connemara is well served by buses which pass very close to the granite hills in the south, the Maumturk Mountains, the Twelve Bens and Joyce's Country. One service travels via Oughterard, Maam Cross, Maum Bridge (Joyce's Country), Leenane, Salruck Cross (at the northern end of the Inagh Valley), Kylemore and Letterfrack to Clifden. Another service reaches Clifden via Oughterard, Maam Cross, Recess and Ballinahinch (Benlettery Youth Hostel). A third service takes a route to the east of Lough Corrib via Headford, Cross, Cong, Clonbur, Cornamona, Maum Bridge and through to Clifden.

From Westport a bus route skirts the southern edge of the Nephin Beg Range via Newport, Mallaranny, Achill Sound and Keel to Dooagh which is in easy striking distance of Croaghaun and Slievemore. Another service allows the west and north slopes of Mweelrea to be approached via Murrisk (Croagh Patrick) and Louisburgh, ending at Killadoon.

While these routes should not change to any great extent, times certainly will, particularly between summer and winter schedules and so it is wise to check with Bus Eireann before you finalise your travelling arrangements.

Accommodation is plentiful in the summer with many country houses, guest houses, hotels and hostels (An Oige and independent) offering good facilities at reasonable rates. However, from October to Easter many of the smaller establishments close and so it is necessary to check with the Tourist Board which guest houses and hotels will provide accommodation for winter walkers.

The Burren is well served by hotels and guest houses in Lisdoonvarna, Ballyvaughan and Kinvarra and bed and breakfast is available at many houses along the main roads. Irish cottages are available for rent at Corrofin. There is a youth hostel in a fine setting at Doorus (353 121) to the northwest of Kinvarra and independent hostels at Fanore (133 068) and Doolin (0797). It is advisable to book your hostels in advance, particularly in the summer, because they are very popular with all types of out-door enthusiasts. There are sites for camping and caravanning at Fanore and Doolin on the west coast of the Burren.

The Galway-Spiddle-Inveran road offers plenty of bed and breakfast accommodation for those who wish to explore the granite hills. Oughterard also offers various types of accommodation, including an independent hostel, and good access to the hills and to the fishing on Lough Corrib. Maam Cross, Recess and Roundstone offer bed and breakfast accommodation and there are facilities for campers and caravaners at the latter village. There is an An Oige youth hostel at the foot of Benlettery (770 484) which is an ideal base for exploring the Twelve Bens. Clifden, Letterfrack, Tullycross and Rinvyle are all well geared for visitors and at Tullycross the modern Irish cottages in the centre of this attractive village are very popular throughout the year. The youth hostel at Gubbadanbo (770 649) is in a most beautiful setting at the mouth of Killary Harbour and just a

7

boat ride from Connaught's highest mountain, Mweelrea. But it is a bit off the beaten track — so hitchhikers, be warned and give yourselves plenty of time to reach the hostel. Leenane offers a range of hotel and bed and breakfast facilities. There are several guest houses in and around Maum. Cornamona, Clonbur and Cong are all well equipped to serve the walker.

Westport, Louisburgh and many small villages south of Clew Bay offer various types of accommodation as do Newport, Mallaranny and several of the villages on Achill Island. There is a youth hostel (732 959) on the west side of Corraun Hill, overlooking Achill Sound. There is a new hostel at Treanlaur Lodge beside Lough Feeagh. Bed and breakfast is offered at several houses on the rather desolate Mallaranny-Bangor Erris road and also by the roads on the north and east flanks of the Nephin Beg Range. The youth hostel at Pollatomish (826 365) is well situated for those wishing to explore the north Mayo coast and the Mullet. Clare Island offers guest house, hotel and hostel facilities.

There are very few organised camp sites in the region and in fact there are very few ideal sites for camping near the mountains of Galway and Mayo because the land is so wet and boggy. However, where suitable sites occur on private land permission for short-term camping is usually readily given in anticipation of considerate and responsible behaviour on the part of the camper.

Geology

The uplands and mountains of western Ireland provide as rich a variety of geology, scenery and walking conditions as could be desired in such a small area anywhere in Europe. The angular limestone bluffs of the low Burren hills contrast strongly with the rounded granite hills on the north side of Galway Bay. These, in turn, are dwarfed by the quartzite peaks and ridges of the Twelve Bens and the Maumturk Mountains. The various sedimentary rocks of Mweelrea, Joyce's Country and the Partry Mountains create yet another type of mountain scenery, perhaps less harsh than their southern neighbours, but just as dramatic. The Nephin Beg Range, whilst of similar geology to the Bens has a different character again, rising as it does from the largest blanket bog in Ireland.

The geological history of the region belongs to three main phases. Firstly, the Precambrian era which pre-dates about 600 million years ago when little life existed and virtually no fossils were preserved to facilitate the dating of rocks. The Twelve Bens, Maumturks and the Nephin Beg Range originated during this era. Secondly, the Palaeozoic era, which followed the Precambrian and lasted over 350 million years. It is represented by the Ordovician and Silurian rocks in north Galway and south Mayo and the Carboniferous limestone in the Burren, as well as the Galway granites which may be of Devonian age. Thirdly, the recent Pleistocene epoch, during which extensive ice sheets played such an important role in shaping the present-day scenery.

The oldest rocks in the region form the highest mountains. The Dalradian quartzites of Precambrian age form the peaks and ridges of the Twelve Bens, the Maumturk Mountains, the Nephin Beg Range, Nephin and Croaghaun and Slievemore on Achill Island, and the north Mayo cliffs. Croagh Patrick is another quartzite peak but it was formed later during the Silurian period. The quartzites originated as clean sandy sediments which spread out on the sinking floor of a shallow sea. Heating from within the earth and pressure from overlying deposits metamorphosed the quartz sands into quartzites. The finer particles which were deposited as muds during the same period were changed to schists. Originally the schists were protected by the more resistant quartzites on top, but eventually these were breached by erosive agents and the weaker schists were denuded more rapidly to form the lowlands which flank the major ranges today. Prominent white quartz veins are regular features of the Connemara schists as these quartzites and schists are generally collectively called and blue dolomite bands are not uncommon. However, most notable of the minor rocks associated with the schists is the green Connemara marble which was metamorphosed from an ancient dolomitic limestone. This serpentine rich decorative stone occurs at Lissoughter, at the foot of Derryclare and is still quarried near Streamstown, to the west of the Bens. The Galway granite is younger and was intruded into the crust 400 millions years ago; it covers about 1,300 square kilometres (500 square miles) in a wedge shape extending from Galway City westwards to the southeastern shores of Bertraghboy Bay. It terminates abruptly at the northern shore of Galway Bay, but it is thought by some geologists to continue southwards under the limestone of the Aran Islands and the Burren.

The granite hills are generally lower and of smoother profile than those of Donegal, for example, and only on the western fringe does the ground exceed 300m/1,000ft (Shannamona, 347m/1,138ft; Lackadunna, 323m/1,060ft). There are no large exposures of granite, as elsewhere in Ireland. The range thus has little or no attraction for rock climbers. Furthermore, the impermeability and shallow slope of the parent rock ensures that the overlying peat remains wet for most of the year, making walking conditions generally unpleasant.

Most of the rocks forming the lower hills of the northeastern Maumturks, the southern border of Killary Harbour, Mweelrea, the Sheeffry Hills, Joyce's Country, the Partry Mountains and Clare Island are sedimentary, having been deposited within an ancient sea, the Iapetus Ocean, 600–400 million years ago. Sandstones, grits, mudstones, shales and conglomerates make up the Silurian deposits which rest unconformably on Connemara schists in a band running south of Killary Harbour — with the exception of Rosroe peninsula and Bencraff (555m/1,822ft) — and extending eastwards from Gowlaun to the Maum Valley, terminating on a line linking Leenane and Tonalee (489m/1,606ft). Here faulting has caused a break in the belt, which continues its eastern progress from a point west of Kilmeelickin and south of Bunnacunneen (580m/1,902ft) to its termination at the shore of Lough Mask.

Ordovician rocks predominate north of a line running eastward from the mouth of Killary Harbour, taking in Rinavore (430m/1,409ft), Lough Nafooey and Derry Bay on Lough Mask. Mweelrea, Connaught's highest peak, is part of a syncline composed mainly of resistant grits 1,500–3,000m/5,000–10,000ft thick with some slates, conglomerates and volcanic material. It is separated from Ben Gorm and Ben Creggan by the Bundorragha Valley which marks a zone of faulting which was more susceptible to denudational forces than its surroundings. But the deep and dramatic Glenummera Valley, which winds its way between Ben Creggan and the Sheeffry Hills, is the product of erosion of the less resistant Glenummera slates which surface in the northern limb of the Mweelrea syncline. The slates continue north-eastward in low relief along the northern edge of the Partry Mountains which are an extension of the Mweelrea grits. The Sheeffry Hills are composed of grits similar to those of Mweelrea, but since they are older and were subjected to tighter Caledonian folding they are recognised as Sheeffry grits. To the north these are faulted against the Silurian quartzites of Croagh Patrick; the small granite outcrops forming the hills of Corvockbrack (392m/1,287ft) and Knockaskeheen (392m/1,288ft) southeast of Louisburgh are of Devonian age and intrude the Ordovician and Silurian rocks of south Mayo.

The youngest rock in our region is the Lower Carboniferous limestone of the Burren (*Boireann*, Rocky Place) which is about 300 million years old. The Burren is a dissected plateau of predominantly bare, angular limestone, covering over 260 square kilometres (100 square miles) in northwest Clare. From its northern boundary on the shores of Galway Bay the limestone dips gently southwards until it disappears under the Upper Carboniferous black shales and flagstones of south Clare, roughly on a line running through Kilfenora and Corrofin. Its western boundary is the Atlantic Ocean and to the east its limits are sharply defined by the cliffs of Slievecarran (327m/1,073ft) and the outlying peak of Mullaghmore (191m/627ft) which overlook the limestone plain of Gort. The latter hill shows some of the only folding of limestone in the Burren.

Its highest point is Slieve Elva (346m/1,134ft) in the northwest corner. This summit, like Poulacapple to the east, is composed of Namurian shales and flagstones which are the remnants of a more general cover which was removed mainly by pre-glacial denudation. It is on these impermeable peat-covered rocks that the few surface water courses found in the Burren flow, only to disappear suddenly down swallow holes on reaching the underlying limestone. Otherwise, most of the drainage flows underground, generally in a southerly direction, the Caher River being the only exception, flowing northwest to the sea, mainly on the surface, through its valley of glacial drift.

Burren limestone is of marine origin, massively bedded, extensively jointed and over 900m/3,000ft thick in places. The ice-scoured surface appears to have been barren throughout recorded time, although human activity may have accelerated the removal of whatever thin soil existed in some areas.

Although not strictly part of the Burren, the Cliffs of Moher, 11km/7miles southwest of Lisdoonvarna, are a sight that visitors to the area should not miss. About 10km/6miles in length, they rise 200m/650ft vertically out of the sea at O'Brien's Tower. They are also of Namurian age and the products of a giant late Carboniferous delta. From a base of shales they rise through horizontal beds of sandstone and flagstone to a sandstone platform capped by black Moher shales, just below the car park.

An overwhelming factor in the moulding of the scenery we see today was the work of the Pleistocene ice-sheets which covered much of the west of Ireland a million years or so ago. Centred on the highest peaks in Connemara and Mayo the ice plucked out the rockbound corries that grace their eastern and northern faces today. The glaciers polished the slopes of the hard quartzite peaks, ground down the less resistant granite hills, planed the Burren limestone and gouged valleys out of the softer schists and slates. They carried Connemara rocks in many directions, some granite boulders as far as Mallow and Portarlington. They created lateral moraines in the valleys and on their retreat left terminal moraines, for example, southeast of Maam Cross, west of Kylemore, in the Erriff Valley, swarms of drumlins in the Maam Cross-Clifden corridor and around Tully Cross and an esker north of Ross Lake. A glance at the OS maps will indicate that the major corries in all the western mountain ranges face somewhat between north and east; the possible reason being that, if today's prevailing south-westerly winds occurred during the Pleistocene, snow would have been blown off the tops onto these slopes and fed developing corrie glaciers which would have been hidden from the warming effects of the sun. This hypothesis is certainly true today because the irregular snowfall we do receive only hardens and remains for any length of time in these corries, where snow climbing is an occasional luxury not to be missed. The action of the ice on the granite hills was very severe and gave rise to the highly polished, stony region that is south Connemara today.

In the Burren the ice-sheets probably played a large part in the creation of the limestone pavements and also in the deep glacial grooving which is found along its northern edge. Certainly, the Connemara glaciers left their visiting cards in the form of erratics which occur occasionally on the north slopes of the Burren hills and more rarely on the upper plateau.

Flora and Fauna

The geology and climate of the west of Ireland have created a variety of contrasting habitats which provide a wealth of interest for both amateur naturalists and professional biologists. The high peaks and ridges of Connemara and Mayo, regularly lashed by strong winds and rain, support very few resident plants and animals. But the lower slopes and the intervening bogs, pastures and lakes sustain a considerable diversity of species including several notable rarities. In contrast to the acid soils of Galway and Mayo the lime-rich habitats of the Burren carry a flora which is, in many ways, unique in Europe and its rare flowers and invertebrates attract naturalists from many parts of the world.

Flora   The highest summits of Connemara and Mayo are largely devoid of all but the hardiest vegetation such as St Patrick's cabbage (*Saxifraga spathularis*), the lichen Cladonia and some primitive club-mosses *(Lycopodium)*. In the Twelve Bens it is only on Muckanaght, where the more hospitable schist rises to its summit, that we find a continuous carpet of vegetation to over 600m/1,970ft. Here there are several rare alpine plants such as alpine meadow-rue (*Thalictrum alpinum*), purple saxifrage (*Saxifraga oppositifolia*), mountain sorrel (*Oxyria digyna*), alpine saw-wort (*Saussurea alpina*), dwarf mountain or least willow (*Salix herbacea*) and holly fern (*Polystichum lonchitis*).

The Ordovician and Silurian sediments of Mweelrea, the Sheeffry Hills and the Partry Mountains provide a slightly richer habitat for plants than the quartzite mountains and are well clothed with species such as deer-sedge (*Scirpus caespitosus*), cotton grass (*Eriophorum sp.*) and woolly hair-moss (*Rhacomitrium lanuginosum*) on the higher ground, ling (*Calluna vulgaris*) and mat-grass (*Nardus stricta*) on the upper steep slopes along with purple moor-grass (*Molina caerula*), and heather (*Erica*) where there are rocky outcrops and unimpeded drainage. On the middle slopes bent grass (*Agrostis tenuis*) dominates the flora along with heath grass (*Sieglingia decumbens*) and mat-grass. On the lower slopes, where the soils are richer and drier, bracken (*Pteridium aquilinum*) and the grass *Holcus* are prominent, but where the ground is wet and peaty, ling, purple moor-grass and rushes (*Juncus*) dominate with the colourful bog-asphodel (*Narthecium ossifragum*) coming in on the flatter ground.

The schist, which forms the lower slopes of the Bens and the Maumturk Mountains, is overlain in the valleys by thick deposits of boulder clay and peat. Here, in addition to the ling, sedges and grasses mentioned earlier one can find orchids (*Dactylorhiza sp.*), bog pimpernel (*Anagallis tenella*), milkwort (*Polygala serpyllifolia*), holly (*Ilex aquifolium*), rowan or mountain ash (*Sorbus aucuparia*), a variety of mosses and liverworts and the fascinating insectivorous butterworts (*Pinguicula spp.*).

In contrast to the broken outline and varied shades of grey, green, brown and red of the northern mountains the low granite hills of south Galway create a monotonous vista dominated by purple moor-grass and ling on the drier slopes with cotton-grass, deer-sedge and black bog-rush (*Schoenus nigricans*) on the wetter peat, particularly in hollows left after turf cutting. A tramp across these hills is brightened only by the occasional clump of St Dabeoc's heath *(Daboecia cantabrica)* with its large purple bells and the sparkling clumps of gorse parading along distant roadside verges.

The blanket bogs of southwest Galway and south Mayo are dominated by purple moor-grass, with bog myrtle *(Myrica gale)* and extensive carpets of bog-moss *(Sphagnum spp.)*. In areas where the rainfall is considerable and the soil water has probably never receded from the peat surface there may be an abundance of black bog-rush and often also the white beak-sedge *(Rhynchospora alba)*. In the permanently wet areas, which may be vestiges of old lakes, one finds species such as common reed *(Phragmites communis)* and reed ho *(Menyanthes trifoliata)*.

Notable rarities of Mediterranean-Lusitanian origin occur at several sites in the two counties, in particular in the vicinity of Roundstone. Mediterranean heath *(Erica erigena)*, Mackay's heath *(Erica mackaiana)* and the previously mentioned St Dabeoc's heath all occur in this area. And not far away pipe-wort *(Eriocaulon aquaticum)* and the slender naiad *(Najas flexilis)*, both species of North American origin, grow in shallow bog lakes.

Nowadays western Ireland is noticeably lacking in trees so it is refreshing to tarry awhile near the luxuriant sessile oakwoods *(Quercus petrea)* of Kylemore, sadly threatened now by the spread of rhododendron *(Rhododendron ponticum)* which is springing up in many areas of Connemara and rivalling the splendid fuchsia *(Fuchsia magellanica)* which was also introduced as a hedgerow plant in some places. Oakwoods also survive in several other localities, including Salruck and at the foot of Derryclare.

Among the prominent species growing on the lake islands of Mayo and Galway are the sessile oak, holly, rowan, yew *(Taxus baccata)*, birch *(Betula pubescens)* and common sallow or sally *(Salix atrocinerea)*. Among the 170 or so species of vascular plants recorded on the lake islands the regularly occurring species include St Dabeoc's heath, bell heather *(Erica cinerea)*, ivy *(Hedera helix)*, honeysuckle *(Lonicera periclymenum)*, bramble *(Rubus fructicosa)*, bilberry/blaeberry/whortleberry *(Vaccinium myrtillus)*, greater woodrush *(Luzula sylvatica)*, common violet *(Viola riviniana)*, broad buckler-fern *(Dryopteris dilatata)*, royal fern *(Osmunda regalis)* and bracken.

Moving to the Burren we enter a botanical world almost as bizarre as the landscape which nurtures it. Here the mild, moist atmosphere keeps frost at bay and, along with the good drainage of the fissured limestone, this karst landscape provides a meeting place for plants of Lusitanian-Mediterranean and Arctic-Alpine origin. If the latter plants, in ordinary Irish conditions, attempted to spread to sea-level they would be smothered by the normal summer growth of native stock. But in the Burren exposure to strong winds, heavy rainfall and grazing have contrived to hold back the native plants to allow survival of the arctic-alpines such as mountain avens (*Dryas octopetela*). These grow in close proximity to such species as the delicate maidenhair-fern (*Adiantum capillus-veneris*), a native of warmer and moister climates, but now a common resident of limestone crevices.

But, of course, the Burren supports more than the well-publicised rarities and over 600 flowering plants as well as many lower forms occur in its varied habitats.

The common and widespread species include the prominent bloody cranesbill (*Geranium sanguineum*), its close relative herb-Robert (*Geranium robertianum*), and the little, white burnet rose (*Rosa spinosissima*) which is a woodland relic occurring wherever the soil is shallow, but also sometimes with ling on considerable depths of peat. The carline thistle (*Carlina vulgaris*) is also abundant, particularly on the limestone pavement, on thin grassland and on the coastal sand dunes. Other species in this category include white flax (*Linum catharticum*), bird'sfoot trefoil (*Lotus corniculatus*), hawthorn (*Crataegus monogyna*) which is common in thickets and scrub and as an invader of undergrazed pasture, woodruff (*Galium odoratum*), the eyebrights (*Euphrasia spp.*) wild thyme (*Thymus praecox*) growing in small hummocks, hazel (*Corylus avellana*) which is the dominant tree over wide areas, blue moor-grass (*Sesleria caerulea*) in all grasslands where grazing has not been too intense, early purple orchid (*Orchis mascula*), sweet-scented orchid (*Gymnadenia conopsea*), the rare close-flowered (Irish) orchid (*Neotinea maculata*) of Mediterranean origin and several species of the *Dactylorhiza* orchids.

Species which tend to be restricted to limestone pavement include stone bramble (*Rubus saxatilis*), hoary rock-rose (*Helianthemum canum*), rue-leaved saxifrage (*Saxifraga tridactylites*), white stonecrop (*Sedum album*), an escape which has successfully invaded the pavement, usually close to its garden of origin, wall pepper (*Sedum acre*), northern bedstraw (*Galium boreale*), ash (*Fraxinus excelsior*) and blackthorn (*Prunus spinosa*), both of which are usually found in a prostrate form, and, finally, bracken.

The limestone crevices (grikes) provide interesting habitats in which the following species are often found: tutsan (*Hypericum androsaemum*), which is a characteristic crevice plant but usually very undersized in this habitat, holly, madder (*Rubia peregrina*), salad burnet (*Sanguisorba minor*), sycamore (*Acer pseudoplatanus*), spleenworts (*Asplenium spp.*), hart's-tongue fern (*Phyllitis scolopendrium*) and the maidenhair fern mentioned earlier.

Mountain avens are abundant and dominant over wide areas but are generally more plentiful at higher altitudes, although they tend to be replaced on the highest grounds by bearberry (*Arctostaphylos uva-ursi*). Finally, juniper (*Juniperus communis*) is abundant but only locally distributed while yew occurs frequently on cliffs and pavement, but always as isolated trees.

And one last word on mountain plants. They appear at their best in their natural setting. Please leave them there for others to enjoy.

Fauna   The fauna of the west of Ireland is generally less well known than the flora. Animals do not lend themselves to study as easily as plants because of their mobility and their secretive and sometimes nocturnal behaviour. For obvious reasons there is probably more known about the larger vertebrates — the fish, birds and mammals — than the invertebrates, with the possible exception of the butterflies and moths of the Burren. Little is known about the animal communities which occupy the various habitats in the region so it will be necessary to describe the fauna in more general terms than the flora.

Butterflies are probably the most attractive and popular terrestrial invertebrates and we are fortunate that the Burren is Ireland's Mecca for lepidopterists. Here twenty-six of Ireland's thirty-three species have been recorded since 1960.

The pearl-bordered fritillary (*Clossiana euphrosyne*) is one of Ireland's rarest butterflies and occurs only in the Burren. At the other end of the scale the Irish subspecies of meadow brown (*Maniola jurtina*) is one of the most widely distributed species in Ireland and occurs in Connemara and much of Mayo as well. The speckled wood (*Pararge aegeria*), the wall brown (*Lasiommata megera*) and the dark green fritillary (*Argynnis aglaia*) are all reasonably common and widespread in the Burren, less common on Connemara, scarce in the Mayo uplands and unrecorded in the granite hills of south Galway. The ringlet (*Aphantopus hyperantus*) is widely distributed throughout the Burren and the lowlands of Galway and Mayo, but is fairly uncommon. The little blue (*Cupido minimus*), the wood white (*Leptidea sinapsis*) and the dingy skipper (*Erynnis tages*) seem to be restricted mainly to the Burren and a narrow corridor extending into central Galway.

The most widely recorded species in the upland areas of Galway and Mayo (which are also present in the Burren) are the grayling (*Hipparchia semele*), the small heath (*Coenonympha pamphilus*), the small tortoiseshell (*Aglaise urticae*), the peacock (*Inachis io*), the common blue (*Polyommatus icarus*), the green hairstreak (*Callophrys rubi*), the green-veined white (*Artogeia napi*) and the orange tip (*Anthocharis cardamines*).

It would seem that most of these species were recorded on low ground, but evidence from other parts of the country indicates that butterflies do travel at higher elevations, so walkers should be watchful for these delightful animals in the hills.

The moths and, to a lesser extent, the micro-lepidoptera, of the Burren have been well studied, as have several other insect groups and interested walkers are recommended to consult the *Irish Naturalists' Journal*, the *Proceedings of the Royal Irish Academy* and the *Entomologists Gazette* for authoritative accounts of these.

Ireland is not well endowed with amphibians, but two of the three recorded species have been observed in the west. The third, the rare natterjack toad (*Bufo calamita*), occurs only in west Kerry. The common or smooth newt (*Trituurs vulgaris*) is under-recorded but thought to be widely distributed while the familiar frog (*Rana temporaria*) is common and widely distributed throughout the region. In spring tadpoles can be found in abundance in such widely differing habitats as small rock pools high on the exposed Burren limestone, elevated peaty ponds and well vegetated forest drains in Connemara and Mayo.

Ireland is similarly poor in reptiles and the common or viviparous lizard (*Lacerta vivipara*) is the only species present. It is found in the three western counties but, like the common newt, it is under-recorded and, no doubt, walkers will find it at many new sites in the region.

The fish fauna of the west of Ireland is fairly impoverished, but what it lacks in quantity it displays in quality. The Burren, drained mainly by underground water courses, is not the most interesting stamping ground for an icthyologist although he/she may chance to meet migrating eels (*Anguilla anguilla*) in some subterranean streams. On the other hand the streams and rivers which rise in the mountains of Connemara and Mayo are well endowed with sedentary brown trout and migratory sea trout (*Salmo trutta*) and salmon (*Salmo salar*), all highly prized by anglers. But in such grand company we should not forget the diminutive minnows (*Phoxinus phoxinus*) and three-spined sticklebacks (*Gasterostreus aculeatus*) which inhabit the slower reaches of some of our mountain rivers, as do eels and ever wily pike (*Esox lucius*). However, most interesting from the point of view of mountain and moorland ecology are the char (*Salvelinus alpinus*), arctic relics which inhabit the deep, cold waters of many western loughs. They are relatively small, non-migratory relations of trout and salmon which feed mainly on plankton. Once fairly widespread, their range is now being reduced partly, at least, by pollution.

The most common bird in the hills is the meadow pipit (*Anthus pratensis*) with its thin but distinctive call. This is followed by the skylark (*Alauda arvensis*) which enlivens the mountain air with its hovering flight and familiar song. But, perhaps the most regal of our mountain birds, is the raven (*Corvus corax*) with its slow wing beat and its deep raucous call. It is a common sight throughout the region where it nests on steep mountain crags and coastal cliffs. It is one of our earliest breeders, sometimes laying as early as the end of February. The raven's smaller cousin, the chough (*Pyrrhocorax pyrrhocorax*), is most common around coastal cliffs, such as Moher, but it does breed in the mountains of Connemara, and it is not uncommon for its high-pitched call to echo across the hillsides, directing one's eye to the brief flash of its characteristic red legs and bill. Its much maligned relation, the hooded or grey crow (*Corvus corone cornix*), is common throughout the hills and if one can forget its tarnished image one will find a most impressive and attractive bird.

The kestrel (*Falco tinnunculus*), hovering in search of prey, is a familiar sight throughout the region whilst the smaller merlin (*Falco columbarius*) is restricted mainly to Connemara and southwest Mayo. The sparrowhawk (*Accipiter nisus*) is typically a woodland bird but it has adapted to the more open habitats of western Ireland and is fairly common. But perhaps the most uplifting sight and the most stirring sound echoing through the rockbound valleys is the scream of the peregrine (*Falco peregrinus*) which, fortunately, seems to be holding its own in the region.

The red grouse (*Lagopus lagopus*) is a bird of the heathery hillsides, but like the heather on which it depends for food and shelter it is becoming scarce. Similarly, the corncrake (*Crex crex*), a summer visitor to hayfields and rushy pastures, is disappearing fast as farmers turn from hay cutting to early silage making. Golden plover (*Pluvialis apricaria*) breed in small numbers on the bogs and hillsides of Connemara and Mayo. These, too, along with the merlin, are seriously threatened by the afforestation and cutting of our bogs. The colourful wheatear (*Oenanthe oenanthe*) is one of our commonest summer visitors, arriving sometimes as early as mid-March and staying until October. Flitting around the shores of many of our moorland lakes each summer will be one or more pairs of common sandpiper (*Actitis hypoleucos*) and nesting on the islands a few pairs of common gull (*Larus canus*) or black-headed gull (*Larus ridibundus*) and the occasional pair of mallard (*Anas platyrhynchos*) or teal (*Anas crecca*).

In winter one will sometimes flush snipe (*Gallinago gallinago*) and woodcock (*Scolopax rusticola*) from the hillsides, but once the frosts come they tend to retire to the lower ground. Greenland white-fronted geese (*Anser albifrons flavirostris*) winter in small numbers in the region and may be seen flying in formation between their roosts on some mountain top lakes and their feeding grounds in the valleys. Other winter visitors to our western lakes include the majestic whooper swan (*Cygnus cygnus*), the pochard (*Aythya ferina*) and the occasional goldeneye (*Bucephala clangula*).

Among the remaining residents the stonechat (*Saxicola torquata*) is very common and is often seen perching on telephone lines running through the valleys. The dipper (*Cinclus cinclus*) is a secretive bird of the fast-flowing mountain streams, where a brief glimpse of one bobbing on a rock or flying low over the water will be as much as many walkers can hope for. Then, on the lakes, the tiny dabchick, or little grebe (*Tachybaptus ruficollis*) is a common sight, as is the grey heron (*Ardea cinerea*) silently stalking its prey at the water's edge.

Turning to the mammals of the mountains it is safe to say that the fox (*Vulpes vulpes*) is the most noteworthy. Unfortunately, the badger (*Meles meles*), with its low profile and distinctive shuffle, is largely nocturnal and although it is probably as common, if not commoner than the fox in some areas, it is rarely seen, except all too often as a corpse on the roadside. Likewise, the otter (*Lutra lutra*) is scarcely seen because of its quiet and secretive habits, but, like the previously mentioned species, it is fairly common throughout parts of Connemara and Mayo but, no doubt, less common in the waterless areas of the Burren.

The Irish hare (*Lepus timidus*) is fairly widely distributed throughout the west but it is not encountered as often as one might like. Rabbits

(*Oryctolagus cuniculus*) are still fairly common in the west of Ireland, but nowhere near as plentiful as they were before the introduction of myxomatosis which, although not rampant today, does recur in many localities at intervals. They are particularly abundant on the more fertile hills of Joyce's Country and on the limestone pastures of the Maumturk Mountains. The Irish stoat (*Mustela erminea hibernica*) is an elusive animal but perhaps commoner than generally realised and, with a bit of luck, it can be seen throughout the area.

The pine marten (*Martes martes*) is a shy, retiring animal and is one of Ireland's rarest mammals. It is similar in form to a stoat or ferret but is larger and has a bushy tail. As its name suggests it is generally arboreal, but it has adapted to more open, rocky terrain and the Burren is one of its main strongholds in the country. It also occurs in the wooded areas to the west and north of Lough Corrib and in similar habitat in Mayo. Also rare and restricted to Clare, Galway and Mayo, is the lesser horseshoe bat (*Rhinolophus hipposideros*). Finally, the largest mammals to be encountered in the west are the feral goats (*Capra sp.*) which roam the Burren plateau, the hills around Killary Harbour, Joyce's Country and several other areas in Galway and Mayo in herds of up to several dozens, eking out a living on the steep rocky hillsides where the sheep cannot go.

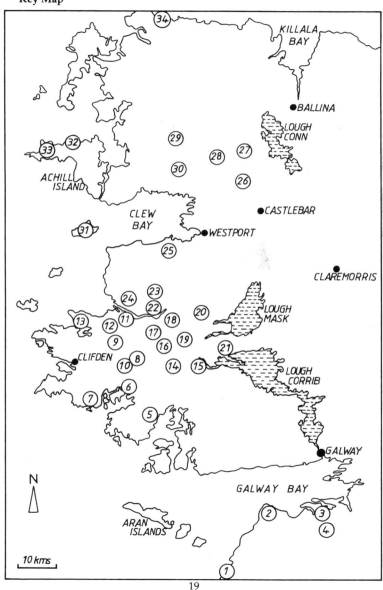

1. THE CLIFFS OF MOHER

The cliffs of Moher are one of the most spectacular sights in the west of Ireland. Their magnificence is enhanced by the surprise they bring to the unsuspecting traveller approaching from the landward side. The cliffs are 10km/6miles long and rise vertically about 200m/650ft to their highest point in horizontal strata of shales, flagstones and sandstones.

Unfortunately there are now some problems with walking the cliffs. Farm fences have been erected quite close to the cliff edge so that walking on a windy day is quite dangerous. Also some farmers resent walkers and occasionally have turned them back. But the cliffs are so wonderful that I do not want to discourage you completely. Perhaps the best suggestion is to go to the well-signposted Visitor Centre on the Liscannor-Lisdoonvarna road (R478) and walk either northwards via O'Brien's Tower or southwards towards Hags Head until the windy weather, a human agency or your own wishes call a halt! Even if you go no further, the view from the top of the cliffs a few minutes' walk from the Visitor Centre is well worth the trip. For the brave who dare the whole cliff walk, a description follows.

Starting from Fisher Street you join the cliff top track at 068 963 near Castleview Guest House. The cliffs open up ahead of you and Crab Island and Doolin Pier come into view to your right. The ascent is easy but involves crossing the occasional stream, wall and electric fence on the way. Take a detour to the cliff edge every now and again to see the 'text book' stratification and folding of the rocks below. To the north of Luogh, hidden by an earth bank topped by a barbed wire fence, is a deep chasm — Poulnagavaul (*Pol na Gabhal*, Crooked Inlet). Here the sea has attacked a weakness in the cliff and carved out a deep inlet bounded by vertical, iron-stained rock faces and steep grassy slopes above. Southwards, beyond Luogh the track passes closer to the cliff which, during the breeding season, is occupied by fulmars, kittiwakes, guillemots, razorbills and, on top of some of the lower buttresses with their growth of natural vegetation, puffins — a taste of some of the ornithological delights to come.

Leave the track where it turns south-eastwards and head for the cliff edge and the steep climb to the highest point of the cliffs between Aillenasharragh and O'Brien's Tower. Take great care along this section and keep well away from the edge which, in places, is crumbly. The story of Cornelius O'Brien and his activities on and around the Cliffs of Moher is presented in several publications available at the Visitor Centre at the east end of the car park.

A few hundred strides beyond the car park will take you out of earshot of the razzmatazz of the visitors' area (threatened by further undesirable development at the time of writing) and you will be able to resume your walk in the true ambience of the cliffs.

The rhythm of the cliff top is broken in places by old quarry workings, reminders of a flourishing industry which employed over five hundred men last century. Otherwise, it is easy going to Hags Head with its early nineteenth-century signal tower. This was erected on the site of an Iron Age promontory fort, built about 2,000 years ago.

Northwards from Hags Head the graceful sweep of the cliffs carries your eye to the bare, limestone terraces of the Burren. To the south you can see Mutton Island, Loop Head and the mountains of Kerry on a clear day.

From here you can move southwards along the cliff to the first quarry where a track will take you back to the minor road and on a route parallel with the cliffs towards the car park or eastwards to Liscannor.

Distance: Fisher Street to Hags Head, 10km/6miles. Ascent: 200m/650ft. Walking time: 3 hours.

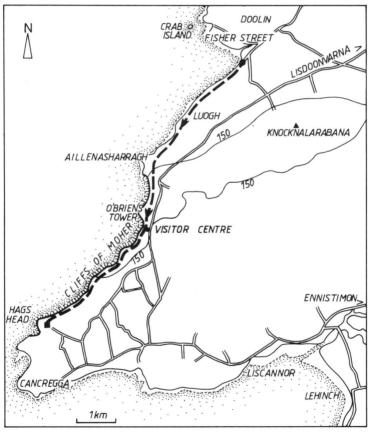

Reference OS Maps: Sheets 51 and 57 (1:50,000).

2. GLENINAGH MOUNTAIN AND BLACK HEAD

This is a long but fairly easy walk taking in the hills and the coast. It is an excellent introduction to the Burren, a unique limestone karst area whose flora is internationally famous.

Park near a walled-off, disused quarry on the south side of the R477, to the west of Gleninagh Castle (*Gleann eidhnach*, Ivied Glen). Return towards the castle and about 100m/110yds before a cottage on the sea side of the road pass through a farm gate on your right and walk southeast across the small field to a gap in the hedge which is the start of the track which will take you over the col between Cappanawalla and Gleninagh Mountain. The track is narrow and rough in places but the going is easy and the views of Galway Bay, Connemara and north Clare are very pleasing. To the east the extensive sand and mud flats of Ballyvaughan Bay are exposed at low tide and it is here that many migrating birds fuel up in spring and autumn on their way to or from their breeding grounds. It is here, also, that Brent geese, all the way from Arctic Canada, spend their winter months.

The track winds up the hill to the col, short heather and bracken on each side. As you cross a wall at the top of the col a broad vista of bare, terraced limestone cradling extraordinarily lush pastureland and hazel scrub opens up before you. This rich valley is a surprising and heartening sight in an otherwise barren expanse of rock. Follow the track into the valley, passing the low remains of a ring fort to your right, skirting along the east side of the walled fields (where the track fizzles out) until you sight the first cottage, where you can join a more substantial track leading to Feenagh. Here, take the track to your right up the hill. This is now part of the Burren Way. From the col you will be able to look up the Caher Valley to the important caving areas centred on Polnagollum (*Poll na gColm*, Hole of the Doves) and Pollelva (*Poll Eilbhe*, Hole of Elva). Downstream you will catch a glimpse of Galway Bay between the hills. Your track continues on the opposite hillside, walled on both sides, and unusually wide.

At the summit you'll come upon an ancient stone ruin (*Cathair an Aird Rois*) comprising an outer wall and two inner buildings, commanding a fine view of the Caher Valley and Galway Bay.

Descend between the neat and tidy hay fields to a gate. A right turn and then a left will bring you to the river and then to the continuation of your track. A short cut down the valley and across the col between Gleninagh Mountain and 319m/1,045ft would bring you back to base quickly if you wished to curtail your journey.

Otherwise, climb the track from the partly derelict village of Formoyle to the summit plateau from where you will be able to appreciate the uniform height and the rounded profile of the Burren as you look back across your route. To the south the shale summit of Slieve Elva, rich in vegetation, stands out in a sea of limestone.

A wall blocks the path near the summit and it is a convenient place to decide whether to continue to Ballyelly and the castle or leave the track and head north-westwards to Murroogh. If you choose the latter route be careful of the broken ground, so well camouflaged by heather, and the series of steep scarps which may be circumvented if found to be too difficult to descend directly. If you follow the natural line you will meet the road at the church and then the main road which will take you round Black Head, past the lighthouse and back to base. Or, by taking the first track to the right you can join the old road which will take you at a higher level (and away from the traffic) around Black Head to a point about 1km/1,100yds west of your starting point. The start of the old road is opposite a new bungalow and overgrown with bushes for the first few metres. Likewise, there is dense scrub at the end of the road, requiring you to make a short detour.

Distance: 17.5km/11miles. Ascent: 460m/1,500ft approx. Walking time: 5–6 hours.

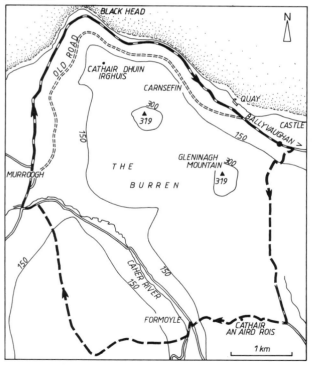

Reference Maps: OS Sheet 51 (1:50,000) or The Burren (1:35,000).

3. ABBEY HILL

One of the most pleasant short walks in north Clare is across the bare limestone of Abbey Hill, returning to base along the old road which runs parallel to the main road (N67 from Kinvarra to Ballyvaughan) about 60m/200ft above it.

Start about 400m/440yds from the eastern end of the old road at 312 105 taking the natural line up the rocky ramp to the shoulder, where the gradient eases.

The undulating Slieve Aughty Mountains form the eastern horizon as they rise out of the fertile lowlands of southeast Galway. These blend into the highly indented coastline of inner Galway Bay with its small bays and inlets, many of which harbour the renowned Galway Bay oysters. The muddy inlets also provide good feeding grounds for wintering ducks, geese and waders.

Tawin Island divides the inner bay into two increasingly distinct bays — quiet, unspoilt waters to the south and bustling waters around Galway where commercial and recreational boating activities are increasing apace.

The narrow coastal band on the north shore, with its small fields and its regrettable ribbon of housing, stretches from Galway to Inveran against a backdrop of bleak moorland and granite hills.

In the foreground is Aughinish Bay (*Each inis*, Horse Island), with the remains of an ancient tide-driven mill on its northern shore. The tides rush backwards and forwards through the narrows at Newquay at anything up to three metres per second (six knots). In summer its narrow fertile southern hinterland presents a rich mosaic of yellow cereals and bright green pasture.

Muckinish Bay (*Muic inis*, Hog Island), with the castle at its narrow entrance, comes into view, with Ballyvaughan Bay and Black Head in the background. Across Galway Bay the bogs of Connemara stretch away to the Bens in the far distance.

From the summit there is a magnificent panoramic view of the Burren. If you cross the wall and descend the slope to the southwest for a short distance you'll see the impressive ruins of Corcomroe Abbey (*Corco Mruad*, [territory of] The Descendants of Mruad), a Cistercian Abbey founded in 1180 by Donal Mor O'Brien, King of Limerick.

Return to the wall and follow the northern branch down towards the old road, taking care where the ground steepens briefly. On reaching the old road you can either return to your starting point, passing St Patrick's Well (*Tobar Phadraic*) on your right or continue westwards to the main road at St Patrick's Church.

Distance: 5.5km/3.5miles. Ascent: negligible. Walking time: 1¼ hours.

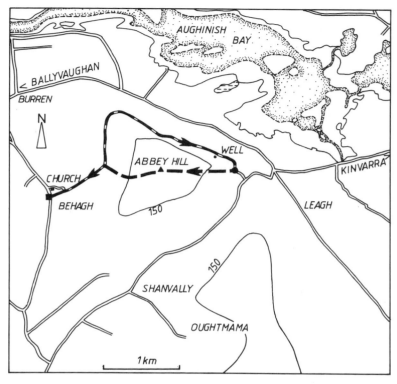

Reference Maps: OS Sheet 51 (1:50,000) or The Burren (1:35,000).

4. TURLOUGH HILL AND SLIEVECARRAN

Leave the Kinvarra-Ballyvaughan road (N67) at the crossroads east of Abbey Hill, take the minor road southwest to Turlough and then take the first turning left and then left again towards Aghawinnaun. Stop short of the first farmhouse and park at the side of the road (296 050).

Pick a route across the bare limestone towards the craggy slopes of Turlough Hill (282m/925ft) and to the right of a small triangular wood. As elsewhere in the Burren the limestone is broken and loose, so care should be taken when negotiating the bluffs. You are surrounded by typical Burren scenery, grey limestone terraces rising up to broad rounded summits, the uniformity broken here and there by patches of dark green heather or hazel and some bright green pastures where thin soils have survived to nurture the grass.

The summit cairn is soon reached and provides a good vantage point from which to take stock of the surroundings. Muckinish Bay lies between Moneen Mountain and Abbey Hill and, beyond Finavarra Hill, Galway Bay reaches over to the lowlands of Connemara. Below you, Corcomroe Abbey sits at the foot of Abbey Hill and in the foreground is Oughtmama, the site of an early monastery associated with St Colman (*Ucht Mhama*, Breast of the Pass).

As you traverse the ridge, Aughinish Bay and Kinvarra Bay, with their broken and irregular shorelines, come into view, with Kinvarra at 'the head of the sea' drawing one's eye over the plains of east Galway. Follow the sweep of the ridge down to the col, past an early Iron Age ring fort to your left, and then Carn Bodhar on the way up to the summit of Slieve-carran with its flat and monotonous top. If you continue eastward you will come upon Eagles Rocks, a line of steep cliffs overlooking extensive limestone pavement on which is perched the ruins of the tiny oratory of St Colman guarded by thick hazel and bramble scrub. You may be lucky-enough to spy a herd of feral goats which eke a living from these barren hilltops.

Following the top of the crags will turn you onto a westerly course and to the summit of Gortaclare Mountain (*Gort a'Chlair*, Field of the Plain) from which you will be able to descend with relative ease to your starting point, watching out for cliffs on the way.

Distance: 10.5km/6.5miles. Ascent: 460m/1,500ft. Walking time: 4 hours.

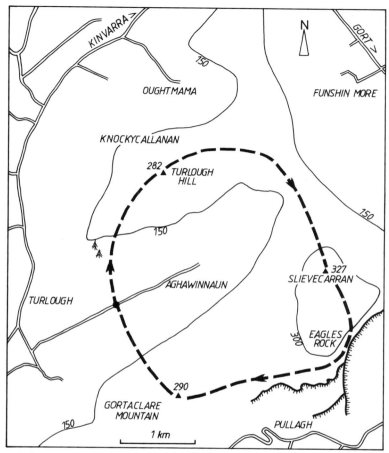

KINVARRA

N

GORT

OUGHTMAMA

150

FUNSHIN MORE

KNOCKYCALLANAN

282
TURLOUGH
HILL

150

150

AGHAWINNAUN

327
SLIEVECARRAN

TURLOUGH

300

EAGLES
ROCK

290

GORTACLARE
MOUNTAIN

150

1 km

PULLAGH

Reference Map: The Burren (1:35,000). [90% of the walk is on OS Sheet 51 (1:50,000).]

5. DERRYRUSH TO KILKIERAN RIDGE

If one wishes to combine the pleasures of hill walking with those of beachcombing, then the ridge from Derryrush (Doire Iorrais, Peninsular Wood) to Kilkieran village (Cill Ciaran, Church of Ciaran) can provide the answer.

Start at the minor crossroads on the R336 (895 385) at Derryrush. Take the lane north-westwards to a point where you can move onto the hill and up the slope by the large, rectangular water tanks. Follow the obvious dry line up towards the main ridge which sweeps off ahead of you to Kilkieran. Sedges give way to heather and bog myrtle on the dry patches, and gorse, resplendent in May and June against a rather uniform background, flourishes on the extra dry outcrops. The ascent is easy going if you keep to the rocks and dry ground. There are plenty of short granite slabs, boulders and crags on the route which will provide welcome diversion for the inveterate scrambler.

From the first plateau at 300m/1,000ft the Aran Islands will be seen guarding the entrance to Galway Bay and beyond them the sharp outline of the Cliffs of Moher standing firm against the Atlantic swell. To the east the incongruous turf-burning electricity generation station (no longer operating) at Screeb suddenly reduces one's feeling of remoteness. Kilkieran Bay, with its multitude of islands and shoals, is the home of a flourishing oyster fishery and now also the site of intensive salmon-rearing operations.

As you reach the crest of the ridge, the grey expanse of the Maumturk Mountains erupts from the flat corridor of bog and water below you. In autumn the red of the purple moor grass of the bog contrasts vividly with the stark backcloth of grey quartzite. The uniformity of the low ground is broken only by the small lake islands with their richer vegetation which has been spared the recent depredations of man and his livestock. From the high point of the ridge (355m/1,164ft) one can compare the high jagged tops of the Bens with the smoother peaks of the Maumturks which, as C.W. Wall has pointed out, 'look as if their tops have been knocked off and strewn along the edges'. Between the two mountain ranges the Inagh Valley directs one's view northwards to the Mweelrea Mountains. Then, to the east of the Maumturks, the upper reaches of Lough Corrib come into sight, cradling the richly wooded Hill of Doon.

The ridge is generally wet and can be hard going in places. In the past, it must have been an arduous task to transport turf from the now derelict turf banks which flank the ridge. At the col the ground slopes smoothly westwards down to the bog, but the descent is steep and craggy to Lough Aconeera, where good numbers of wildfowl will be seen in winter. It was near this point that I once flushed eight grouse, an all too rare sight these days.

Beyond the summit (341m/1,120ft) it is possible to take a short cut back to the road via the turf cuttings before the plantation. However, the route above the plantation, which has been partially replanted after a fire a few years ago, is easy and leads to a rough track which joins a metalled road running down to Kilkieran, with its pub, shops and seaweed factory. A five-mile stroll along the road or shore will bring you back to the starting point.

Distance: 11.5km/7miles; plus walk of 8km/5miles, back to start. Ascent: 460m/1,500ft approx. Walking time: 4 hours; plus 2 hours for walk back to start.

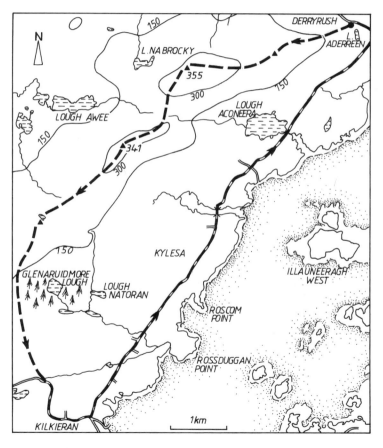

Reference Maps: OS Sheet 44 (1:50,000) or Connemara (1:63,360).

6. CASHEL HILL

Cashel Hill (312m/1,024ft) is an isolated mound overlooking Bertraghboy Bay. It is an igneous intrusion of dark gabbroid rocks, considerably older than the lighter, neighbouring lowland granites. It is difficult to reach from the picturesque village of Cashel (Caiseal, Fort) with its delightful church and pier and its two fashionable hotels. It can be approached from the road junction (R340/R342) at 818 422 along the ridge but this is a rather long walk for such a small peak.

A more direct route starts at Scrahalia, 787 431 on R342, just to the west of the little pier. Take the track beside a line of young lodgepole pine trees past a new house, cross the gorse-covered pasture and climb a wire-topped fence onto open ground. Proceed to the ridge ahead of you and follow it to the final steeper summit ascent, taking any of the grassy gullies to the prominent nick just below the peak.

From the summit there is a spectacular view of the Twelve Bens, the Glencoaghan Valley, the Inagh Valley and the Maumturks. Below you to the northwest, the woodlands of Ballynahinch stand out like an oasis in a desert of bog, rock and water. To the east and the west you are dazzled by countless glistening lakes, many with islands of luxurious vegetation, relics of better times.

The sheltered waters of Bertraghboy Bay are outlined in various shades of seaweed brown and orange.

Return by more or less the same route, perhaps taking a more southerly line to enjoy a full view of the sea.

Distance: 3km/2miles. Ascent: 300m/1,000 ft. Walking time: 1½ hours.

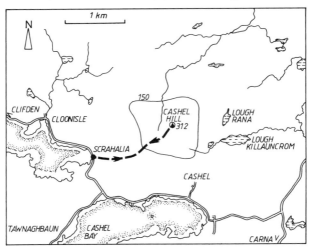

Reference Maps: OS Sheet 44 (1:50,000) or Connemara (1:63,360).

7. ERRISBEG

Errisbeg (Iorrus beag, Small Western Peninsula: 301m/987ft) is a low hill to the west of the attractive village of Roundstone. It is sometimes called Roundstone Hill by those under the misapprehension that there is a relationship between the village name and the shape of the hill. In fact the Irish name for the village is Cloch na Ron, Seal Rock.

The hill is accessible from the coast road (R341) from Roundstone westwards, but taking a route from any point within three miles of the village involves the negotiation of many stone walls — with the attendant dangers of annoying the land owners by knocking down the walls, and of injuring oneself in the process. Therefore, I prefer to start to the west of the hill, at a sharp bend in the road at 684 397, just before a quarry on the south side of the road. Here there is parking space and access to open ground through a gate.

Take any route past the lake and up to the summit ridge, picking your way carefully through the crags and angular boulders. There are three summits on this very entertaining ridge with its small gorges, crags and sheltered hollows. Return by the same route.

I cannot but agree with many other authors who consider the view from Errisbeg one of the finest in the region — the Bens, Maumturks, the lakes, the coastline, the scatter of offshore rocks and islets, and Clifden with its two prominent spires. To the south is the classic tombolo, composed of the shells of countless microscopic animals, which joins a low granite island to the shore, forming Gorteen Bay (*Goirtín*, Little Garden; also known as *Port na Feadoige*, Plover's Shore) and Dog's Bay to the west.

I would find it hard to recommend a better short hill walk in the whole region.

Distance: 3km/2miles. Ascent: 240m/800 ft. Walking time: 1½ hours.

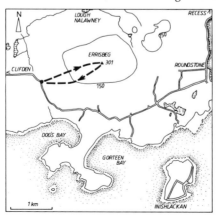

Reference Maps: OS Sheet 44 (1:50,000) or Connemara (1:63,360).

8. DERRYCLARE-BENCORR HORSESHOE

The Derryclare-Bencorr Horseshoe is one of the most enjoyable introductory routes in the Twelve Bens. Follow the R344 from Recess towards Kylemore and park at the entrance to Derryclare Wood at 846 499.

Take the forest road, bearing left at a fork, for about 2.5km/1.5 miles to the end where there is room to park several cars. Retrace your steps for a few yards and take the ride on your left (830 506) between stands of lodgepole pine and a few sitka spruce and over a rocky knoll.

On emerging from the plantation, where the ground begins to steepen as the rock changes from schist to quartzite, take the gully leading up towards the summit of Derryclare (*Doire an chlair*, Wood of the Plain or of the Plank: 677m/2,220ft). The gully is often dry in summer and usually not very wet in winter and offers easy, but entertaining, scrambling. The gully peters out as the ground levels off at about 370m/1,200ft to give easy walking over short heather on springy turf until the easy slabs leading to the summit are reached. These slabs, like the gully, can be avoided if necessary.

The ridge incorporates a sharp knoll which leads to a steep rocky descent to the col followed by an ascent of about 150m/500ft over broken rocky ground to the large cairn on the summit of Bencorr (*Beann Corr*, Peak of the Conical Hill: 712m/2,336ft).

From the summit you can return to the Inagh Valley via the eastward running spur, ensuring that you descend to low ground both before reaching the nose of the spur which is steep and treacherous, and early enough to be able to skirt the recent planting which is encroaching on the end of the spur. Or you can continue to Bencorrbeg (582m/1,908ft) along the ridge, descending to the valley at the end of this spur where the ground is somewhat easier than that directly below the minor summit.

Throughout the walk you are continually stimulated by fine views but none can compare with that from Bencorrbeg of the entire sweep of the walk just completed. The picture of the sharp ridge, the deep corries and the steep, rocky spurs leaves one with a feeling of deep satisfaction.

From the foot of the Bencorrbeg spur, head towards the near corner of the plantation, where you will meet a short ride which will take you to the forest road and thence back to your starting point.

Distance (long route): 9.6km/6miles. Ascent: 900m/3,000ft approx. Walking time: 5 hours.

Distance (short route): 6.4km/4miles. Ascent: 840m/2,750ft approx. Walking time: 4 hours.

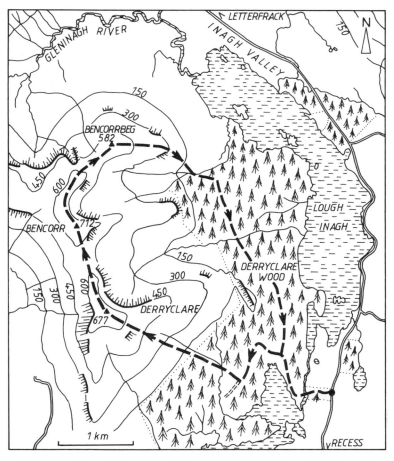

Reference Maps: Mountains of Connemara (1:50,000) or OS Sheet 37 (1:50,000).

9. MUCKANAGHT AND BENBAUN

This walk will take you to the hub of the Bens. At the northern end of the Recess-Kylemore road (R344), take the westward road below Barnaheskabaunia, cross the new bridge and park near the start of the rough track which runs parallel to the Kylemore River. It leads eventually to one of the most isolated habitations in the area, at Glencorbet.

Take the track to its end point at the farm and continue along the bank of the river where the ground is moderately dry. To your left the bog extends to the foot of the Knockpasheemore-Benbaun ridge but to the right it has been transformed into a sea of green conifers.

Follow the line of the left fork of the stream to the col between Benbrack (*Binn Bhreac*, Speckled Hill) and Muckanaght (*Meacanach*, Place of Lumps and Ridges: 654m/2,153ft). The dryish ground gives way to eroded and very wet peat, but contemplation of the ancient stumps of 'bog deal' revealed by the erosion should take your mind off any brief discomfort. What was this valley like when it was forested? Which animals inhabited the forest? Could 'prehistoric climbers' have penetrated the forests to reach the summits of the Bens? Will future climbers be able to reach the peaks once current planting schemes are complete?

Muckanaght rises to your left, steep, smooth and green in contrast to its grey, craggy neighbours. It is the most inaccessible of the Bens and is probably one of the least visited of the group. From the col the summit is reached by a route starting at an obvious ramp between two small crags. Care should be taken because the ground is steep and the short vegetation is often greasy.

From the summit there is a fine all round view of Connemara. Looking down on the col from which you ascended you will notice that the northern face is craggy. This, along with other crags, is shown on the *Mountains of Connemara* map, but the OS map (although the contours are superior) shows neither this, nor any of the numerous other crags in the Bens and Maumturks.

Descend to the next col with caution and take the easy ground to the minor summit of Benfree (638m/2,093ft) and then follow the curved ridge to the scree-bound peak of Galway's highest mountain, Benbaun (*Beann ban*, White Mountain: 729m/2,395ft). It is the hub from which all the main ridges of the Bens radiate and it rightly commands one of the most comprehensive views in the whole region.

Return via the ridge leading to Knockpasheemore (*Binn Charrach*, Rock-encrusted Peak) and descend to Glencorbet by the small stream flowing from the minor col below the knoll of 456m/1,500ft.

Distance: 10.5m/6.5miles. Ascent: 870m/2,850ft. Walking time: 5–5½ hours.

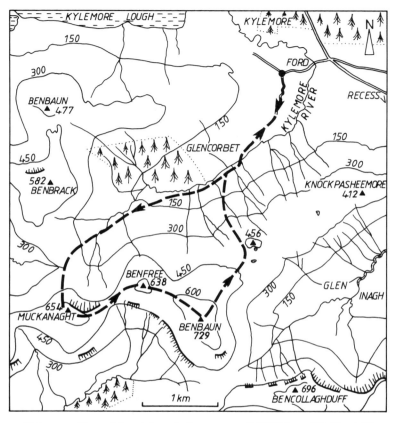

Reference Maps: Mountains of Connemara (1:50,000) or OS Sheet 37 (1:50,000).

10. THE GLENCOAGHAN HORSESHOE

The Glencoaghan Horseshoe takes in the six peaks of Derryclare (677m/ 2,720ft), Bencorr (712m/2,336ft), Bencollaghduff (698m/2,290ft), Benbreen (694m/2,276ft), Bengower (666m/2,184ft) and Benlettery (580m/ 1,904ft). It is one of the best-known and most popular walks in Connemara, particularly with walkers staying at Benlettery Youth Hostel.

It makes little difference whether you do the walk clockwise or anticlockwise. However, I prefer to start at Derryclare because when I come off the last peak, Benlettery, perhaps tired and aching, shelter, rest and refreshment can be close at hand. When descending from Derryclare you are faced with a long road walk which can be hard on already sore feet, whereas the same road walk at the beginning of the day serves to warm you up for coming exertions.

From the youth hostel go east along the Recess road (N59) for about 1.5km/1 mile; turn left onto a bohereen, follow it across a bridge and through a farmyard. Leave the road where the slopes of Derryclare loom on your right. The summit can be reached via Lop Rock and the long ridge or, more directly, up one of the steep gullies which rise near the head of the road. The route to the summit of Bencorr is described in Walk 8. From Bencorr, a steep rocky descent brings you onto Devil's Col which overlooks some of the longest rock climbs in Ireland at the head of Glen Inagh. A broad expanse of smooth bare rock eases you into the Bencollaghduff ridge which rises to the summit at 698m/2,290ft and then sweeps down to the col below Benbreen.

From the col, take the southerly ridge leading to the first minor summit of Benbreen. The ground is rocky and heathery and steep enough in places to take one's mind off the strain of the upward slog. And the natural route runs close to the edge of impressive cliffs which plunge almost sheer into the Owenglin Valley — so tread warily. The summit ridge is semi-circular, and beyond the summit of Benbreen (*Binn Bhraoin*: 694m/2,276ft) it leads into a spur which will take you back to Glencoaghan. Therefore it is advisable, particularly in mist, to determine your route to Bengower (*Binn ghabhair*, Peak of the Goat: 666m/2,184ft) with a compass.

The steep descent from Benbreen can be greatly accelerated by a scree run which lands you slightly to the left of the crest of the col. Bengower is steep and steplike and offers good, but generally avoidable, scrambling. From here the walking is easy and once Benlettery (580m/1,904 ft) is surmounted the descent to the hostel, although steep and rocky in places, is quickly achieved.

Distance: 16km/10miles (including road walk). Ascent: 1,500m/5,000ft approx. Walking time: 7½–9 hours.

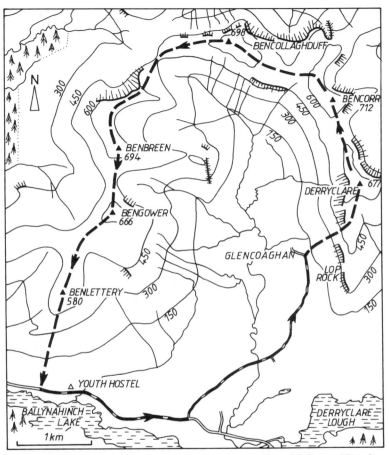

Reference Maps: Mountains of Connemara (1:50,000) or OS Sheets 37 and 44 (1:50,000).

11. BENCHOONA

Benchoona (Binn chuanna, Peak of the Corner: 585m/1,919ft) is one of the nearest hills to the Rosroe (Gubbadanbo; Gob an Dambha, Point of the Spit) Youth Hostel. Start at the bend in the Tully Cross-Leenane road where the bridge crosses the stream flowing from Lough Fee to Lough Muck (Loch Muc, Lake of the Pig) (780 621).

Take the direct route up the steep grassy slope facing you or, if this is too slippery for comfort, as it can be in damp conditions, follow an easier line onto the ridge below the northfacing crags.

Taking the first route you will come to a small plateau at about 120m/ 400ft where you can stop and take note of your surroundings, Inishturk to the northwest, the Maumturks to the southeast, ancient potato ridges to the north of Lough Muck and again on the southwest side of Lough Fee. Below you and to the north there is a ring fort atop a mound — a strategic position overlooking the pass linking Killary Harbour's main pier at Gubbadanbo with the hinterland.

As you ascend the ridge the Inagh Valley, cradled by the Maumturks and the Bens, directs your view across the bogs of Connemara to Galway Bay in the south. And to the north, Mweelrea, Clare Island and the host of rocky islets which break up the Atlantic rollers as they approach the sandy Mayo shore come into view.

To the right of your route the ground steepens into dangerous wet and broken crags which are best left to the agile feral goats which make their living on the high ground.

From the top of the ridge you will be able to look down on Little Killary Bay, with its fringe of oakwoods in the foreground, the small Protestant church and the remarkable graveyard nearby where once it was customary for mourners to smoke clay pipes after burials and then leave them at the grave. The graveyard is well worth a visit just to enjoy the inscriptions on some of the headstones! At the northeast corner of Little Killary you should be able to discern a pillar of rock standing out from the main cliff. This is known as the Pinnacle and, like the neighbouring cliffs, it offers a number of rock climbs ranging from Very Difficult to Very Severe. If you want to develop your climbing skills or experience any other outdoor pursuits you should visit the Little Killary Adventure Centre located at the head of Little Killary Bay.

From the summit plateau you can continue to Garraun (601m/1,973ft) and return via the obvious ridge to the south shore of Lough Fee, or traverse Benchoona and descend the steep northern slope to stepping stones across the river on the seaward side of Lough Muck.

Distance: 5.5km/3.5miles (both routes). Ascent: 600m/2,000ft approx. Walking time: 3 hours.

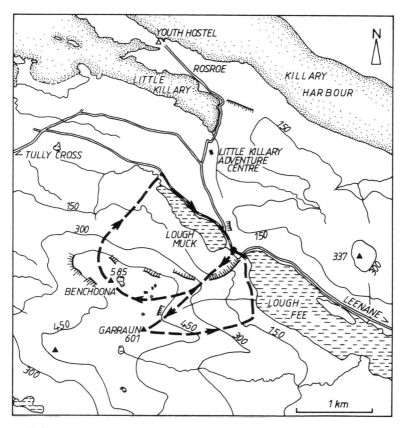

Reference Maps: Mountains of Connemara (1:50,000) or OS Sheet 37 (1:50,000).

12. DOUGHRUAGH

When I first travelled the road (N59) from Letterfrack to Leenane I was taken completely by surprise when I came upon the magnificent edifice of Kylemore Abbey, virtually built into the hillside of Doughruagh, surrounded by oakwoods and overlooking a most beautiful lake. It was built originally by a wealthy Liverpool merchant, Mitchell Henry, in the nineteenth century, but today it is a convent school for girls. At the time of writing there is a charge of £2 for walking on the paths in the Abbey estate, though curiously, car parking is free.

Start from the car park of Kylemore Abbey (*Coill Mhor*, Big Wood). Walk beside the lake in front of the Abbey along a track which joins the main road at the west end of Kylemore Lough. Follow the road for about 100m, then slant left up the hillside along a faint path. When you reach a stream turn left and climb directly to open ground. The mass of Doughruagh is on your left (west). Head directly for it over mixed boggy and rocky ground. Your route crosses an old track and climbs steeply to the summit plateau. This is a wilderness of loughans and rocky knolls, and the summit (529m/1,736ft) is well to the north side.

From the summit there is a less familiar view of the Bens, in which the minor peaks of Little Benbaun (Maolan), Binn Bhreac and Diamond figure prominently, with the main ridges a distant backdrop. Across the bog to the north the surf-edged rocky islets at the mouth of Killary Harbour are backed by the grey-blue shapes of Clare Island and Achill.

On the return journey head directly south towards the hidden Abbey. As you come over the edge of the plateau you will see below you a white statue of the Sacred Heart. Pause for the view — very different from the summit view — of the Kylemore valley, before picking your way carefully down the steep slopes, avoiding the many small crags, to the statue. In 1996 there were some rock slides on the direct descent and it is no longer recommended except for very experienced walkers. Instead, retrace your steps as far as the old track you crossed on the ascent, turn right and follow the track to the statue. From the statue a path leads back through the rhododendrons to the Abbey. Do not attempt to descend anywhere else; you can spend hours forcing your way through the bushes!

Distance: 4.5km/3miles. Ascent: 500m/1,700ft. Walking time: 2½ hours.

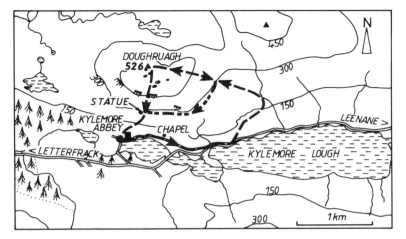

Reference Maps: Mountains of Connemara (1:50,000) or OS Sheet 37 (1:50,000).

13. TULLY MOUNTAIN

Tully Mountain (357m/1,172ft) is the most westerly peak in Galway and, as such, commands a wide range of unique views.

Starting on the road to the north of the summit (672 619) at a point overlooking Tully Lough (*Tulach*, Small Hill) and Tully Cross village with its bright white buildings, take a direct route across the turf banks and up the heathery slope to the large cairn at the summit.

The western aspects of Mweelrea, Garraun and the Bens make a refreshing sight for one who is used to viewing these hills from inland, and the bird's eye view of Ballynakill Harbour resolves at once the contortions of its shoreline which are so difficult to unravel from sea level. The old lobster pond and derelict packing shed on Dawros peninsula are reminders of busier days for west coast fishermen. A clear sweep of the sea takes in all the islands from Slyne Head to Clare Island and Achill.

Tully Mountain would make a fine ridge walk which could be incorporated into a round trip, taking in the seashore, from, say, Renvyle House Hotel or Tully Cross. The mountain can be reached from Tully Cross by a track running south of the Lough.

Distance: 0.8km/0.5miles. Ascent: 270m/900ft. Walking time: 1 hour.

Distance: circuit via Renvyle and Tully Cross, 13km/8miles approx. Ascent: 340m/1,100ft. Walking time: 4 hours.

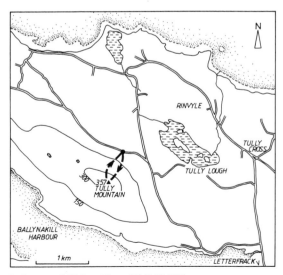

Reference OS Map: Sheet 37 (1:50,000).

42

14. THE MAUMTURKS WALK

Lloyd Praeger, in his classic book The Way that I Went *describes the traverse of the Maumturk Mountains from Maam Cross to Leenane as a 'glorious day's walking'. And so it is. But 24km/15miles of the roughest terrain in the country with about 2,300m/7,500ft ascent (plus 60m/200ft more descent, because the finish is at sea-level) is not an expedition to be taken lightly and walkers are advised to be well equipped and competent with a map and compass. The ridge may look fairly straightforward on the map, but in mist even experienced walkers are known to have gone astray. And remember, if you have to abandon the ridge part way, there is still a lot of ground to cover before you reach base.*

Start from a parking place off the R336 on the Maum side of the Maam Cross — Maum col at 969 496 (not from the new parking area overlooking Maumwee Lough). Walk across the bog towards the high, rounded crags. Move left onto a ramp before you reach the crags and head for an old fence which will guide you to the summit (613m/2,012ft) of Leckavrea Mountain or Corcogemore (*Corcog*). The summit offers a comprehensive view of Joyce's country, upper Lough Corrib and south Connemara.

Continue north-westwards down the ridge, bearing west at the appropriate point to reach the col. To your right a steep rocky corrie drops away into the bog-bound Failmore Valley and to your left a longer, narrower valley plunges down to the forested slopes above Lough Shindilla.

The remains of the fence continue to serve as a useful guide up the steep slope to the west summit (*Mullach Glas*: 624m/2,045ft). From here the going is a bit easier but in misty conditions navigation can sometimes be rather tricky. Continue along the ridge to the third major summit (*Binn Mhor*: 663m/2,174ft) which lies on the south side of the plateau, and bear north-westwards again and descend by the steep spur, aiming to the left of the small lake which lies in a hollow below St Patrick's Bed and Holy Well.

From the col take the steep but easy grassy ridge up to 633m/2,076ft. From here the ridge to 703m/2,307ft is easy going in good weather and provides a commanding view of the Inagh Valley and the Bens. But be careful if mist comes down because it is easy to descend into the Failmore Valley before you reach 703m/2,307ft, without realising your mistake until it is too late.

From 703m/2,307ft descend north-westwards to Loch Mham Ochoige. This is an ideal place to camp if you wish to do the walk in two stages. Cross the col and then take the broken slope westwards to Knocknahillion (607m/1,993ft) taking care to avoid the crags to your right. From the summit there is a fine view of the Inagh Valley and the Lehanagh Loughs in the bog below you to the south. Lissoughter (*Lios Uachtair*, Upper Fort), the site of a now derelict Connemara marble quarry, lies further south while to the west Loughs Inagh and Derryclare are set against a background of dark green coniferous trees capped by the grey ridges of Derryclare and Bencorr.

Turning northwards, descend to the ridge, following its gentle curve westwards past the small lake and then climb to the summit cairn of Letterbreckaun (669m/2,193ft, *Leitir Brecan/Binn Bhriocain*, Brecan's Hillside) which stands out prominently well to the west of the natural route along the ridge. From this vantage point there is a panoramic view of the hills to the north, and to the west Ben Baun can be seen clearly, standing sentinel at the head of Glen Inagh.

Beyond Letterbreckaun the hills change in character and soften somewhat as the geology changes from quartzite to Silurian sedimentary rocks and, underfoot, bare rock and loose boulders give way to springy turf and wet bog. But you still need your wits about you because the ridge winds backwards and forwards between Letterbreckaun and the col at the head of Glenglosh in a way which leads one to underestimate the difficulty of this section. For example, to avoid a deep and dispiriting valley between Maumturkmore (468m/1,536ft) and 356m/1,167ft you are advised to contour the hills northwards from Tober to the col, rather than cross the two summits.

The steep climb up from the col takes you onto a peat-hagged plateau at around 549m/1,800ft. Take a direct route across this towards Leenane, passing the lake on your left and taking care not to venture too close to the cliffs on your right. A steep and often slippery slope brings you down to the road by the Leenane Hotel.

Each year, in early May, the University College Galway Mountaineering Club runs a 'Maumturks Walk' for experienced walkers. It is well organised, with many check points along the route, a mountain rescue team on hand and refreshments at the finish. It is done alternately from south to north and north to south to minimise the environmental effects. Further details can be obtained from the Secretary of the Mountaineering Club, University College, Galway.

Distance: 24km/15miles. Ascent: 2,300m/7,500ft approx. Walking time: 10–14 hours.

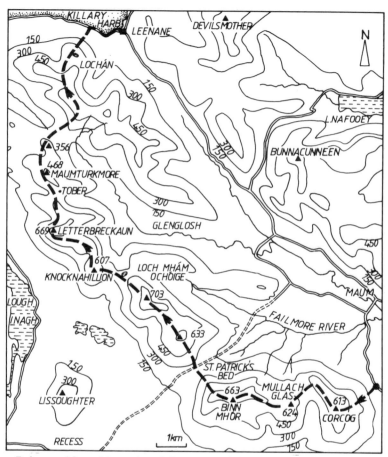

Reference Maps: Mountains of Connemara (1:50,000) or OS Sheets 37, 44 and 45 (1:50,000).

15. LACKAVRA HILL

As you approach Maam Cross from Oughterard, Lackavra (Leic Aimhreidh, Ragged Rock Slab) Hill (398m/1,307ft) is the first hill to come into view. It is in the townland of Leckavrea, unlike its higher namesake to the west which is more correctly called Corcog.

Turn right off the Galway-Clifden road (N59) at Maam Cross and park at a layby just beyond the summit of the col where you have a fine view of the Maum Valley (969 496). (This is not the new parking area overlooking Maumwee Lough.) Across the road, to the east, you will see the foot of a curving ridge which will deliver you right to the summit of Lackavra. Beware of the fence which may be electrified! The climbing is very easy and this route is a fine introduction to the Maumturks which stretch out to the northwest. The summit is rocky, but the crags on the final approach can be circumvented easily.

You will be rewarded with a superb view of the upper reaches of Lough Corrib, including the thirteenth-century keep and curtain wall of the O'Conor Island Castle, Castlekirke (*Cais lean na Circe*, Hen's Castle). To the southeast there is an unimpeded view of the barren granite hills of south Connemara rolling down to Galway Bay and to the northwest the Maum Valley cleaves the stark quartzite peak of the Maumturks from the more hospitable green hills of Joyce's country.

You can return by the same route or explore the eastern slopes of the hill where there were once mine workings, primarily for copper. Due north, across the lake, you may be able to discern the old mine buildings and tailings on the hillside above Carrowgarriff. Alternatively, you can continue southwards along the summit ridge, descend to Maumwee Lough and return along the shore to the col.

Distance 4.8km/3miles approx. Ascent: 300m/1,000ft. Walking time: 2 hours.

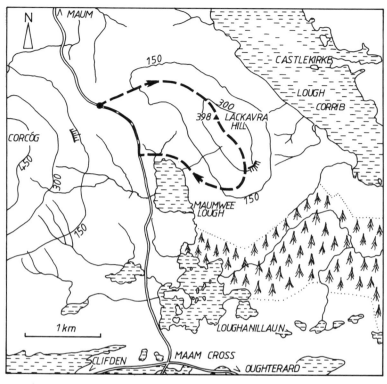

Reference Maps: Mountains of Connemara (1:50,000) or OS Sheet 45 (1:50,000).

16. FAILMORE HORSESHOE

Passing on down into the Maum Valley along the R336 one comes to Teernakill (Tir na Cille, District of the Church) Bridge. From here, looking up the valley of the Failmore River, the next walk can be seen. It is a varied and in places strenuous horseshoe taking in the unnamed Maumturk peaks 633m/2,076ft (Binn Chaonaigh) and 703m /2,307ft (Binn idir an Da Log) before returning via 438m/1,436ft and Knocknagur. (Names are taken from Mountains of Connemara map *by Lynam, May and Robinson.)*

To reach the starting point at the foot of Knocknagur (932 526) (*Cnoc na nghabar,* Hill of the Goats) take the left turn after the school, travel along the Maum Valley 'high road' past the impressive Garda barracks — a reminder of less tranquil times — to Cur (Small Round Hill). Take a sharp turn left up a steep, rough road past prominent limestone crags to the right until the Failmore Valley is visible in front. Park at the layby near the top of the hill — it's difficult to turn further on!

Take the road down to the bridge and cross the Failmore River. Here one is in the heart of perhaps the most desolate valley in Connemara. It is partially filled with glacial drift and is carpeted almost entirely with bog which almost engulfs the two or three fertile pockets that still sustain human habitation.

Several routes can now be selected. Continue up the road towards St Patrick's Well and take the easy grassy ridge up to 633m/2,076ft or, as I prefer, take to the river bank and travel upstream by the ancient potato ridges before cutting off across the fairly gentle, but often wet, rushy slope towards the near buttress which rises to an obvious knoll 614m/2,015ft (*Binn Mhairg*) on the ridge to 633m/2,076ft. Alternatively, for a route demanding greater exertion but which misses the first summit, continue up the valley to the next buttress where one will see a distinct gully offering a more challenging route to the ridge. A rope could be a useful companion here.

The angle steepens considerably where you move onto the quartzite and here may be the last chance to fill water bottles, particularly in summer when the ridge can be very dry. Keep an eye out for the dipper, flitting from rock to rock along the small torrent streams. It is one of the few birds inhabiting these barren slopes.

The ridge from 633m/2,076ft to 703m/2,307ft is easy going in good weather and provides a commanding view of the Inagh Valley and the Bens. Be careful, though, if the mist comes down because it is easy to descend into the Failmore Valley before you reach 703m/2,307ft, without realising your mistake until it is too late.

From 703m/2,307ft descend north-westwards towards *Loch Mham Ochoige,* but, to avoid unnecessary climbing, stop short on the boggy platform above the lake and then pick a safe course down across the scree to the col which forms the head of the Failmore Valley. This is raven country and I have seen six or more perform their raucous antics within a few metres of me. To the northwest is a steep gorge, with vegetation, dropping into the Bealnabrack Valley with strange 'herring-bone' channels marking its right bank. In the opposite direction the head of Lough Corrib appears beyond the sweep of the Failmore Valley.

If tired at this stage you might think it's easier to retreat down the valley. However, the going is difficult and often wet in the valley and not really much better than over the tops and the views are more impressive from the higher ground.

Across the valley the sculptured corries and truncated spurs of the Maumturks ridge illustrate magnificently the powerful action of ice in bygone ages. Bog deal can be found amongst the peat hags on Knocknagur, and descending to base one is pleasantly surprised to find lush swards beneath the limestone outcrops alive with rabbits, including the black variety.

Distance: 12.2km/7.6miles. Ascent: 900m/3,000ft approx. Walking time: 5½ hours.

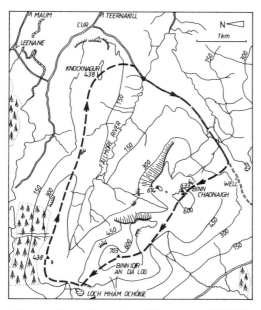

Reference Maps: Mountains of Connemara (1:50,000) or OS Sheets 37 and 38 (1:50,000).

17. CNOC NA HUILLEANN AND BINN BHRIOCAIN

To sample the wild white quartzite summits of the Maumturks without committing yourself to walking the whole ridge, I can recommend this walk which takes you into the heart of the range and has magnificent views of the Twelve Bens across Glen Inagh, as well as vistas of the Maumturks summits stretching away to north and south.

Cnoc na hUilleann (607m/1,993ft) is approached from Ilion West (*An Uillinn Thiar*) on the minor road linking Tullywee Bridge on the Maam Cross-Recess Road (N59) and the Inagh Lodge Hotel. Park at any convenient widening of the road somewhere near 868 524.

Cross the bog and join a stream which flows from the southern flanks of *Cnoc na hUilleann*. Head for the grassy col, passing limestone crags on your left. Amongst these crags are some of the few small potholes in Connemara. To your right bare quartzite cliffs rise sharply, guarding the approach to *Binn Idir an Dá Log* (703m/2,037ft), the highest peak in the Maumturks. At the col there is a lake, L. Mhám Ochóige which marks the crossroads of several routes. It is also an ideal place to camp for anyone taking two days to complete the Maumturks walk. Ascend the broken slope to the summit of *Cnoc na hUilleann* from where you will have a fine view of the Inagh Valley, with Lehanagh Loughs in the bog below you to the south. Lissoughter (*Lios uachtar* the upper fort), the site of a now derelict Connemara marble quarry lies further south while to the west Loughs Inagh and Derryclare are set against a background of dark green coniferous trees capped by the grey ridges of *Binn Doire Chláir* and Binn Chorr.

Turning northwards, descend to the ridge, following its gentle curve westwards, pass the small lake and then climb to the summit cairn of *Binn Bhriocáin* (669m/2,193ft) (Letterbreckaun on the OS map) which stands out prominently well to the west of the natural route along the ridge. From this vantage point there is a panoramic view of the hills to the north and, to the west *Binn Bhán* can be seen clearly, standing sentinel at the head of Glen Inagh.

Return by the same route as far as the first col and descend the steep rocky slope westwards, picking up a stream on your way. This stream will bring you to the Western Way, and after a few minutes walk south along it, to the minor road, and after a further 15km/1mile to your vehicle.

Distance: 8.5km/5.5miles. Ascent 730m/2,400ft. Walking time: 4 hours.

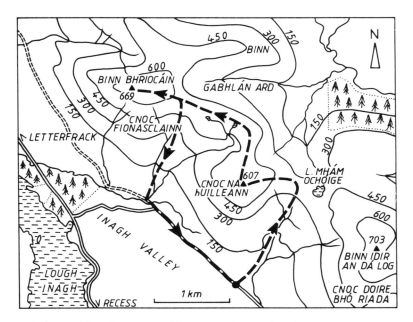

Reference Maps: Mountains of Connemara (1:50,000) or OS Sheets 37.
N.B. Names are from Mountains of Connemara.

18. THE DEVILS MOTHER

This oddly named mountain can be tackled from several angles but I like to approach it from the Leenane-Westport road (N59), just north of Glenane at 912 650.

Start at the foot of a deep gully and pick a route up the steep slope left of the gully to the ridge where a short walk will take you to the minor peak (605m/1,983ft).

From this vantage point the corries of Bengorm can be seen clearly and, to the north, the Sheeffry Hills overlook the headwaters of the Erriff River. From the east three mighty spurs push out from the ice-flattened Maumtrasna plateau, but they are not as rockbound or dramatic as their counterparts on the east side of the range.

An easy ridge walk takes you to the summit of the Devils Mother (650m/2,131ft) where you can rest and absorb the inspiring views of Lough Nafooey, Lough Mask, Croagh Patrick — marked indelibly by the feet of pilgrims — the natural oakwoods at Erriff Bridge and, best of all to my mind, Killary Harbour resting serenely between the opposing giants of Galway and Mayo.

Near the elbow of Killary you might just make out a group of objects floating near the shore. These are mussel rafts which are creating local employment in a reasonably environmentally harmonious way. They are not a beautiful sight, but probably the least of the industrial 'evils' which could afflict the region.

An easy descent along the grassy spur overlooking Glennagevlagh brings you back to the road after your encounter with the Devils Mother — a none too unpleasant experience, I hope.

A more strenuous walk would take an easterly course from the Devils Mother down to the col at 366m/1,200ft and then by the easier ground to 518m/1,700ft, along the county boundary (which, unfortunately, is not marked on the ground!) across the frustratingly broken ground over 622m/2,039ft, 682m/2,239ft, bypassing Maumtrasna on the right and finally descending the westward running rocky spur towards Glenacally Bridge.

Distance (short route): 7.3km/4.5miles. Ascent: 670m/2,200ft. Walking time: 3½ hours.

Distance (long route): 14.5km/9miles. Ascent: 1,000m/3,300ft. Walking time: 6 hours.

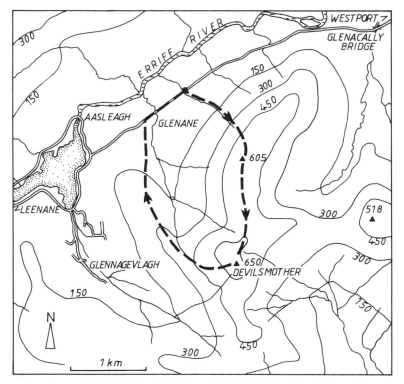

Reference OS Maps: Sheet 37 (1:50,000) plus Sheet 38 (1:50,000) for descent to Glenacally Bridge.

19. BUNNACUNNEEN

Bunnacunneen (Bun a' choinin, *Tail of the Rabbit: 580m/1,902ft*)
contrasts markedly with most of the other relatively high peaks I have
described. It is almost covered in vegetation and has a rounded profile, almost
devoid of rocky outcrops. The most convenient starting point is via the track just
upstream of where the stream from the summit joins the main stream flowing down
to Griggin's Lodge and Pottery at 926 570 (this is the minor road from the Maum
Valley to Lough Nafooey).

I like to follow the stream, with its many small but enchanting
waterfalls, up into the valley rather than take the southern ridge because
when I reach the heart of the valley I feel completely enclosed by
mountains, a pleasant experience not often achieved anywhere else in
Connemara, as a quick glance at the map will show. Even from the heart of
the Bens there is usually a clear view to the neighbouring lowlands.

From the floor of the valley take the right fork to the col and then ascend
the ridge northwards towards the summit. Ahead the Devil's Mother
comes into view and to the south the Maum Valley broadens out as the
Bealnabrack, Joyce's and Failmore Rivers join forces on their course to
Lough Corrib. Across the valley the small, rich, limestone fields of Cur
stand out against their less fertile surroundings.

From the first minor peak the fence will direct you towards the summit.
On your way across the damp, but not unduly wet, peat hags you will have
time to look back at the ruins of Castlekirke perched on an island barely
bigger than itself in the upper arm of Lough Corrib, and north, across the
watershed of Joyce's country, the Drishaghaun Valley will funnel your gaze
to Lough Mask and the lowlands of Mayo beyond. As you approach the
summit Lough Nafooey comes into view and to the west the Bens peep at
you over the Maumturks.

Descend from the summit along the main ridge running south, or take
the steeper westerly slope directly to the road.

Distance: 4.8km/3miles. Ascent: 600m/2,000ft. Walking time: 2¾ hours.

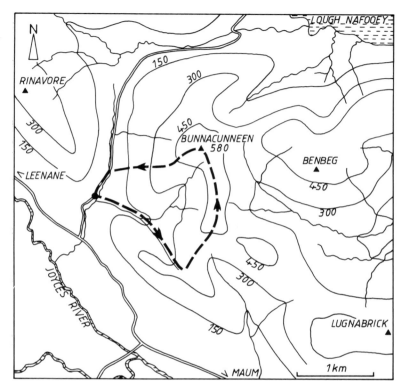

Reference OS Map: Sheet 38 (1:50,000).

20. BUCKAUN

Descending from Maumtrasna (the pass between Lough Nafooey and Lough Mask) on the road to Tourmakeady, take the second turning left to Killateeaun. Continue to the shop/petrol pumps, cross the bridge over the Owenbrin River and take the next turning left, signposted 'Factory'. Bear left at the fork, leaving the tarred road, cross the bridge and continue to the end of the track at the turf banks just short of Dirkbeg Lough (Dearc beag, Small Cave) where the limestone chippings give way to a boulder and sand track.

Had you taken the first turning left along the 'high road' you would have arrived at Lough Nadirkmore, an ideal starting point for a circuit of the southern corrie of Buckaun. However, I prefer to take a more northerly route from the 'low road' (003 657) which offers the possibility of a traverse to Lough Glenawough without too much tramping over bog on the return journey.

Move off southwards across the deep gorge and climb the heathery gully ahead of you to the top of the central spur. The gully is steep in places and can be slippery in wet conditions. From the ridge there is a fine view of lower Lough Mask and its islands. Below you, in the broad valley, the peat-covered moraine is deeply incised by the Owenbrin River and its tributaries. Neat ranks of turf banks are the product of recent human activity which has exposed the many hectares of ancient 'bog deal' stumps, testimony to the valley's wooded past. To the south the two lakes glisten in the early sun, but take on a forbidding air as the sun passes behind the mountains. Together with Dirkbeg Lough these loughs are known as the Dirks and they enjoy a fair measure of popularity with local fishermen.

The ridge is easy going but it narrows and steepens towards the summit and care should be taken in strong winds. To the northwest the familiar face of Croagh Patrick comes into view with the hills of north Mayo in the distance. The single cairn at the top of the ridge is not the summit, but it serves as a useful guide to the exit route down the ridge for those who might find themselves lost in mist on the featureless plateau. The summit is marked by two cairns, a couple of hundred metres to the west.

Follow the rim of the northern corrie northwards across the undulating plateau, over boulder fields and around peat hags, to the precipitous cliffs encircling Glenawough Lough 300m/1,000ft below. The lough is accessible from the northwest but the valley route is always wet and boggy and so the approach from the east is usually more satisfying.

Return either along the northern ridge above the forestry plantation, descending to the valley along one of the fire-breaks or take the steep descent into the Owenbrin gorge and then a short walk over the bog to base.

Distance: 7.3km/4.5miles. Ascent: 490m/1,600ft approx. Walking time: 3 hours.

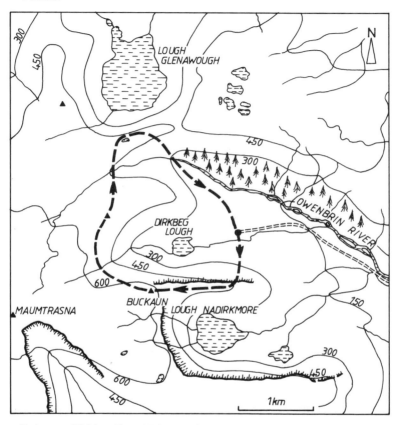

Reference OS Map: Sheet 38 (1:50,000).

21. BENLEVY

Benlevy (Beann sleibhe, Peak of the Mountain: 418m/1,370ft) dominates the isthmus between Lough Corrib and Lough Mask and guards one of the major routes into Connemara from the east. It commands some of the most splendid views in the region which will quickly repay the efforts of any walker who takes on this very modest ascent.

The starting point is some 100 metres short of the end of the minor road from Clonbur which terminates north of Carrick. Taking the road (R345) south out of Clonbur take the first turning right which, although not shown on the map, joins the road skirting the foot of Benlevy. Turn left at a T-junction, signposted 'Ballard', and follow the road past a large new house and then a more modest cottage on the left. A short distance further on there is a track leading on to the hill, beside a stream. There used to be parking space for one car here but at the time of writing there was a small, temporary 'portacabin' at this point so it is wise to check whether parking is acceptable to the kindly lady living here.

Even from the starting point the view of the island-studded upper basin of Lough Corrib is breathtaking. The Dooros peninsula in the foreground projects far into the lough and directs one's gaze over the many islands which are impossible to see in a single sweep from lower ground. The western shore is defined by the granite hills which extend almost to Galway. But the eastern shore merges into the Galway plains which stretch as far as the eye can see.

As you reach the first crest in the path you can look down on the Hill of Doon to the southwest. This wooded knoll, which looks so magnificent from the level of the lough, is now dwarfed against the backdrop of Connemara. The track twists on towards the summit plateau and one wonders why such a track should lead to the top of a mountain. The reason soon becomes plain. Turf was once cut on the plateau where it was stacked against stone walls before being carted down to the lowlands.

A short walk across the peat-hagged plateau will bring you to the summit and a panoramic view of Joyce's country, the Maumturks and the Partry Mountains. To the southwest it is even possible to see Inishmore on a clear day. To the north you have a bird's-eye view of Lough Mask, Lough Carra and the Mayo lowlands.

If you go to the northern rim of the plateau you will be able to look down almost directly into Lough Coolin, partially circumscribed by a track leading to turf cuttings on the northern ridge. On the north side of this lough there are old stone-walled fields, bright green with bracken in mid-summer. You can return by the track or, if you are not restricted in your movements by a waiting car, you may take a leisurely walk back to Clonbur via the northern ridge and Cappaghnagapple (*Ceappach na gcapall*, Plot of the Horses) or via the eastern ridge which brings you back to your original approach road.

Distance: 4km/2.5miles (returning by track). Ascent: 200m/700ft. Walking time: 1½ hours.

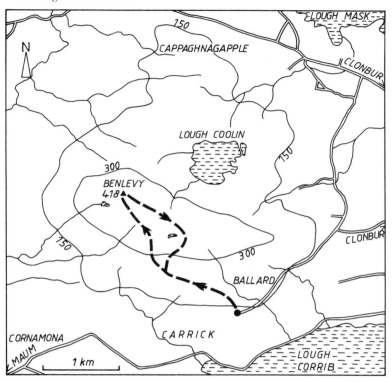

Reference OS Map: Sheet 38 (1:50,000).

22. BEN GORM

Start at the car park on the Aasleagh-Louisburgh road (R335) near the picturesque Aasleagh Falls (895 646) — a place where you might chance to see salmon leaping (Eas liath, Grey Waterfall).

Take the track to the north of the river for a short distance and then cut off up the hill outside the fence past three isolated Scots pine trees.

On reaching the ridge at about 270m/900ft you will gain your first clear view of the steep ice-picked corrie wall with its sparkling stream cascading from the summit plateau to the lake below. To the east the buttress of the Devils Mother marks the beginning of the Partry Mountains which stretch north-eastwards, towering over the Erriff Valley and directing your gaze towards the plains of Murrisk. Beneath you, when the tide is low, the flat sandy expanses at the head of Killary Harbour echo with the calls of curlew, redshanks and gulls. And to the south the little village of Leenane rests comfortably between high hills and deep water.

The ridge steepens as you ascend and drops away sharply to your right into a moraine-filled valley. Ahead, the Kylemore Pass permits a view of the western bogs and the sea on a clear day. But the jumble of summits of the Bens, silhouetted against an afternoon sun, surpasses any other view from Ben Gorm (*Beann Gorm*, Blue Peak).

The summit plateau is fairly level but deep peat hags can make navigation difficult in mist and it is easy to take a wrong and possibly dangerous line of descent. The summit cairn is not actually the highest point on the plateau.

From the summit of Ben Gorm there are several routes by which you can return to Aasleagh. The fit and very enthusiastic may continue to Ben Creggan via the grassy col and past the remains of an old shepherd's hut and then descend the ridge overlooking Glenummera (*Gleann lomaire*, Ridge Glen), returning to base across the lower part of the central spur and nearly two miles of bog — the sort that is none too sympathetic to aching legs. Alternatively, a descent of the steep, narrow central ridge followed by a shorter bog walk can be most rewarding, and certainly less wearing on the temper.

Distance (via Ben Creggan): 10.5km/6.5miles. Ascent: 800m/2,600ft. Walking time: 4½ hours.

Distance (short route): 7.3km/4.5miles. Ascent: 700m/2,300ft. Walking time: 3½ hours.

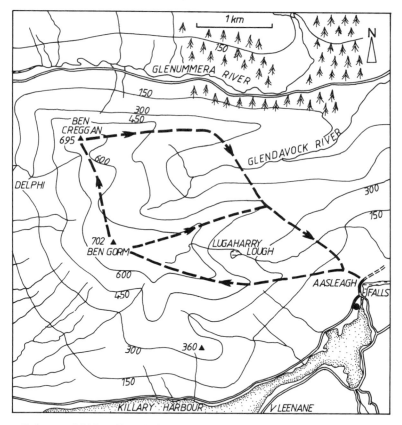

Reference OS Map: Sheet 37 (1:50,000).

23. SHEEFFRY HILLS

I have never felt a great affection for the Sheeffry Hills, largely because every time I have walked them it has rained almost continuously and the miserable feeling thus engendered has been enhanced by the dull walking conditions and monotonous terrain. However, for anyone not afflicted by the same jinx I suggest setting off from the shore of Doolough on the Aasleagh-Louisburgh road (R335) just north of the 'Hotel' (845 678).

The ascent to the summit ridge is uniformly steep, sedgy and slippery in wet conditions. Once on the ridge the going is fairly straightforward although mist can test one's navigation on this rather featureless terrain.

Having studied the map I trust that on a fine day one would have a bird's-eye view of Croagh Patrick, including its summit chapel. And to the south the cliff-girt ridges of Mweelrea and Ben Creggan must be most impressive.

Usually, I have trudged downheartedly to Tievummera 763m/2,504ft and, acknowledging the might of the elements, descended by the western spur, along the eastern edge of the plantation, into Glenummera and returned by the road to Doolough. However, in better conditions I would continue to Tievabinnia 741m/2,429ft and then retire via 529m/1,735ft and the eastern block of conifers to the Glenummera road.

This road was surfaced in the mid-1970s and prior to its upgrading the journey from Doolough to Liscarney was one of the wildest in the area. But the 1980s brought electricity and telephone poles and fencing and these, along with the growth and further planting of monotonous conifers, are all conspiring to suffocate the valley. Any real sense of remoteness has gone, just as it has gone from most parts of Connemara.

I would suggest that the Glenlaur Valley horseshoe, not shown on the map, starting and finishing at Sheeffry Bridge (918 695), taking in 529m/1,735ft, 741m/2,429ft and the northern corries would also provide a good day's walking.

Distance (via 763m/2,504ft): 9.7km/6miles. Ascent: 750m/2,500ft. Walking time: 4¼ hours.

Distance (via 763m/2,504ft and 741m/2,429ft): 14.5km/9 miles. Ascent: 820m/2,700ft. Walking time: 6 hours.

Distance (Glenlaur horseshoe): 10.5km/6.5miles. Ascent: 700m/2,300ft. Walking time: 4½ hours.

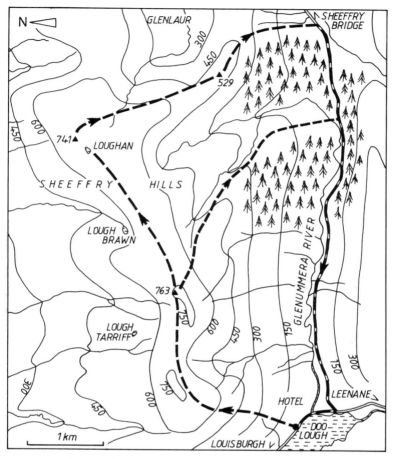

Reference OS Map: Sheet 37 (1:50,000).

24. MWEELREA

Mweelrea (An maol riabhach, *Grey Bald Mountain: 819m/2,686ft) is the highest mountain in Connaught. It provides a variety of climbing and scenery unsurpassed in the west of Ireland. To describe only one route to the summit would do an injustice to this remote grit and sandstone massif, and in mentioning two I am leaving plenty to the ingenuity of the individual walker.*

1. I prefer to do the complete horseshoe from Delphi on the Aasleagh–Louisburgh road (R335), crossing the Bundorragha River 1.2km/0.75 miles north of Delphi Lodge by a foot-bridge which is reached via the south shore of Doolough (there is no access to Mweelrea via Delphi Lodge!). This route leads to steep ground quickly and brings you onto the main ridge early in the climb. In mist be careful not to make the common mistake of taking the spur which runs southeast from Ben Lugmore 798m/2,616ft (unnamed pt 803m on OS map) — it can be a costly mistake on such a long route! The ridge is broad and undulating but to your right the steep cliffs overlooking the Doolough Pass (incidentally, one of the few remaining passes largely unpolluted by electricity wires) may take you by surprise if you are new to the area and relying only on an old map to interpret the scenery. The rest of the walk is simply a matter of following the ridge to the summit of Mweelrea (magnificent panorama of ocean and mountain to west and south) and returning along the undulating southern arm of the horseshoe. Do not be tempted to cut back to your car across the Owennaglogh valley — it is horribly boggy!

2. The most dramatic approach to Mweelrea is via the main corrie on the north side of the mountain. Starting from the north end of Doolough on the R335 to Louisburgh (825 696) cross the stream flowing from Glencullin Lough and then pick up and follow the stream which flows from the valley into the northwest corner of Doolough. At the head of the valley a broad ramp running up to your right above some featureless vertical cliffs leads you to a relatively easy gully which lands you on the main ridge below Ben Bury 796m/2,610ft, a peak which can be circumvented on the way to the summit.

Returning, you can descend by the steep northern spur which leaves the ridge about 100 metres east of Ben Bury. The upper sections are steep and require careful navigation and it is advisable to have a rope at hand (for an ascent as well, if you choose to do this route in reverse). Alternatively, the longer, but technically easier, southern spur via Ben Lugmore will bring you back safely to base, provided you pick a careful route between the crags which litter this part of the mountain.

Whichever route you select to climb Mweelrea, be well prepared for a long hard climb. Give yourself plenty of time for a safe descent in daylight — Mweelrea is a most inhospitable mountain in the dark.

The many crags on Mweelrea offer considerable scope for the rock climber and in the winter the gullies on the north face provide some of the few sites for snow climbing in the west of Ireland.

1. Complete horseshoe
Distance: 15.3km/9.5miles. Ascent: 1,200m/4,000ft. Walking time: 7 hours.

2a. Return by north spur
Distance: 10.5km/6.5miles. Ascent: 900m/3,000ft. Walking time: 5 hours.

2b. Return by south spur
Distance: 12km/7.5miles. Ascent: 1,000m/3,300ft. Walking time: 5½ hours.

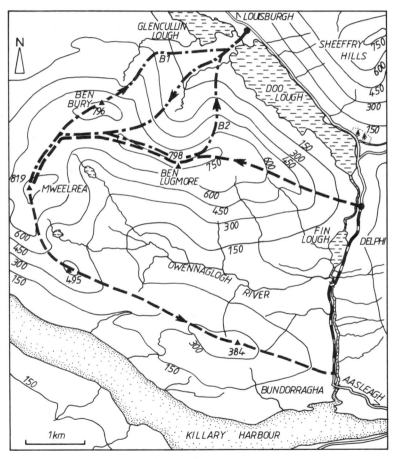

Reference OS Map: Sheet 37 (1:50,000).

25. CROAGH PATRICK

Croagh Patrick, otherwise known as The Reek (765m/2,510ft), is the most climbed mountain in Ireland. Each year on the last Sunday in July thousands of people from all over the country climb the rough pilgrim path to the small chapel at the summit where they pray, hear Mass and receive Communion. In the past most pilgrims made the ascent at night carrying burning torches. But regrettably the Church has stopped this practice, thereby denying us one of the most unusual spectacles to be seen on the western mountains.

The start of the pilgrim path is signposted at 920 824 beside the car park on the Westport-Louisburgh road (R335). On the opposite side of the road, by the sea, is Murrisk Abbey (*Muirisc*, Marshy Seashore). You will require no direction to reach the summit by this route, but take care on the rough rocky track — particularly on the final summit approach where it steepens considerably. I always marvel at the variety of bits and pieces of inappropriate footwear which remain on the track after the pilgrimage — even stiletto heels! But I can only admire the pilgrims who climb The Reek barefooted. If the track isn't to your liking then I suggest that you cut off to the west before reaching the ridge and traverse the heathery hillside to the scree-covered slopes which, with a bit of scrambling, will take you directly to the summit by your own original route.

Alternatively, The Reek can provide an enjoyable ridge walk which will give the walker plenty of time to absorb the magnificent views all around — the bogs and mountains to the south, drumlin-studded Clew Bay and the Mayo mountains to the north and Clare Island, Inishturk and Achill to the west. Continue along the coast road through Leckanvy and turn left at an unsignposted junction with an attractive slate-roofed cottage on the eastern corner (874 820) and opposite a modern house with a slate roof on the sea side of the road. About 1.1km/0.7miles up the road turn left up a rough tarred road, 'elegantly' lined with telegraph poles, towards a small hamlet at the foot of the hill. Take to the ridge where the road bears right (and where you are joined by the electricity poles!), climb to the first peak, thence onto the ridge which leads to the top of Ben Goram (355m/1,164ft) from where you can follow the main ridge to the summit of Croagh Patrick.

Descend by the track to the road, or, after descending the steep section of the track, continue along the ridge and descend the steep spur to the road east of Murrisk (935 823).

Distance: 3.2km/2miles. Ascent: 750m/2,500ft. Walking time: 3 hours.

Whole ridge (excluding return along road): Distance: 8km/5miles. Ascent: 750m/2,500ft approx. Walking time: 4 hours.

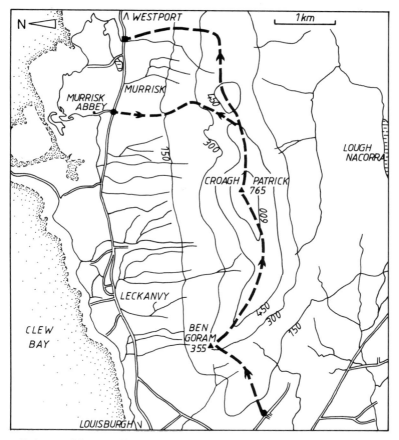

Reference OS Maps: Sheets 30, 31 and 37 (1:50,000). [You can get by on the Pilgrims Path with Sheet 30.]

26. CROAGHMOYLE

*Croaghmoyle (Old Red Sandstone Hill), is a short and easy walk
starting from the R312 on the east shore of Lough Beltra.*

Climb the dry heathery slope to the north of the plantation to the
minor summit of Birreen (Little Hill — more appropriately named than its
neighbour Birreencorragh which is over twice its size). Continue along the
ridge to the summit of Croaghmoyle (430m/1,412ft) where you will find a
transmitter and, what's more, a road leading right up to the summit. But
it would have been unfair to mention that first!

The ridge curves gently westwards down to the shores of Lough Beltra
(*Beal tra*, Mouth of the Strand) with its fringe of green fields. Beyond,
forestry plantations clothe the foothills of Birreencorragh. To the southwest you have a novel view of Clew Bay, looking down onto the 'backs' of
the drumlin islands. The drumlins continue eastwards inland where they
intermingle with many small lakes.

Castlebar, showing signs of urban sprawl, is to the southeast, not far
from Loughs Cullin and Conn. Nephin pierces the sky to the north where
it overshadows its little neighbour Tristia (325m/1,067ft), a rather unusual,
but pleasant name referring, perhaps, to some peculiarity in its shape.

Continue northwards along the ridge and descend by the obvious ridge
towards the north shore of Lough Beltra where you'll meet your road
back to base.

Distance: 8km/5 miles. Ascent: 420m/1,400ft approx. Walking time: 3 hours.

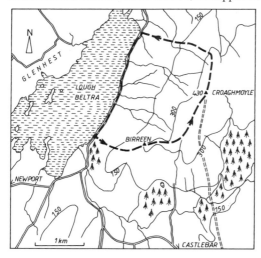

Reference OS Map: Sheet 31 (1:50,000)

27. NEPHIN

Nephin (807m/2,646ft), an isolated quartzite cone, is only 12m lower than Mweelrea and, therefore, the second-highest peak in Connaught. Because of its peripheral location it commands magnificent views of the western mountains and the large lakes, but there its virtues end as far as I am concerned. Its mighty stature is more than outbalanced by the tedious climbing it offers. But don't miss climbing it if you're in the area. And keep an eye out for Pat Coughlan, the local farmer. He is also a walker and a man who appreciates the countryside.

Travelling northwards from the village of Lahardaun on the road to Crossmolina (R315) turn left after 500m/650yds, then left again after a further 1km/0.6miles and travel southwards along the base of Nephin. Start from the end of this fuchsia-lined lane at the foot of the eastern slope at about 125 078. Park in the small layby at the top of the lane and then go on a few more metres and through a gate leading onto the hill. Access to the lower slopes is easy. You can take the direct route to the summit up the long heathery slope between the crags (to your left) and the screes or move further to your left to take the less steep spur. As the ground steepens the vegetation thins out and a fairly direct route to the left of the scree soon brings you to the main ridge. The rock-strewn summit plateau terminates abruptly at its northern rim where ice has gouged out a vast, although not particularly spectacular, corrie. The steep slopes demand a cautious retreat from the summit in misty conditions.

It is not necessary to list the topographical features which can be seen from the summit but I might point out that you will need the 1:250,000 map to help you name all the features you can see from this unique vantage point.

Return by the spur you ascended, taking care to move sufficiently far south to avoid the crags and screes on the eastern slope.

Distance: 6.5km/4 miles. Ascent: 750m/2,500ft. Walking time: 3½ hours.

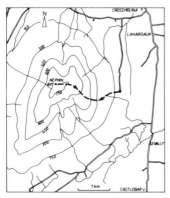

Reference OS Maps: Sheets 23 or 31 (1:50,000).

28. BIRREENCORRAGH

Birreencorragh (Birreen carrach, Rugged Little Hill) is a remote and barren hill. On the map the Birreencorragh group is reminiscent of the Twelve Bens massif — the summit being the hub, with lesser peaks and ridges radiating in all directions into the lowlands.

Travelling northwards from Lough Beltra along the R312 it can be approached by turning left at the crossroads near Keenagh Lodge (040 115). After about 3km/2miles, and just before Keenagh school (021 103) turn left onto a rough tarred road. To the left a river runs through a deep gorge and to the right turf cutting has exposed many stumps of bog pine. Suddenly the road is closed in by heavily grazed, steep, heather-clad slopes as you move into the schist hills of the Birreencorragh. Stop before you reach the green pastures in the river valley and climb the steep heathery slope to the east. Follow the ridge up to the cairn and then move onwards to the summit (700m/2,295ft). Nephin stands alone off to the east, with Lough Beltra backed by Croaghmoyle with its summit transmitter to the southeast. To the northwest stands Nephin Beg and, of course, to the southwest is Clew Bay. Continue round the ridge and descend by the first spur which leads you back into the remote but fertile valley with its small community and the ruins of Glendavoolagh Lodge.

Distance: 8km/5miles. Ascent: 520m/1,700ft approx. Walking time: 3½ hours.

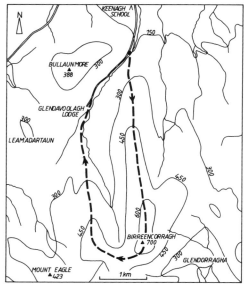

Reference OS Maps: Sheets 23 or 31 (1:50,000).

29. NEPHIN BEG

Nephin Beg (630m/2,065ft) is a fairly inaccessible peak, rendered more so by the vast plantations which have sprung up around its base. However, with a bit of forbearance, it is possible to decipher the maze of forestry roads and find a reasonable route to this imposing peak.

Approaching from Newport on the N59 turn right at the signpost to Furnace (980 940) and travel northwards along the shore of Loughs Furnace and Feeagh, past Srahmore Lodge and into the plantation. Bear left at first fork and then take the first left at the huts and diesel tank, signposted Siuloid Coisabhann, Riverside Walk. The road takes you beside and then over the Altaconey River (*Alt a' gcoinnidhe*, height of the rabbits). Bear left to the end of the road. A short walk over bare peat will take you to a gate, then on to a well-worn track. At the end of the fence move on to 407m/1,336ft, cross the col and, keeping to the higher ground, ascend to the uninspiring summit at Nephin Beg.

The whole of north Mayo spreads out before you, only Slieve Cor (711m/2,369ft) impeding part of the view to the north where blanket bog, punctuated only by the incongruous Bellacorrick power station (*Beal atha an chomraic*, Mouth of the Cord of Combat) and the occasional lake and plantation, stretches into the distance. To the east new plantations criss-crossed with conspicuous forestry tracks dominate the near distance while to the west the lowlands of Ballycroy lead the eye to Blacksod Bay and the impressive peaks of Achill island.

Return to 407m/1,336ft and retrace your steps to avoid getting entangled in young plantations.

Distance: 13km/8miles. Ascent 700m/2,300ft approx. Walking time: 5 hours.

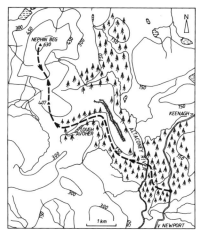

Reference OS Map: Sheet 23 (1:50,000).

30. BEN GORM HORSESHOE

This walk offers the opportunity to enjoy both the remote heights of the Nephin Beg Range and splendid views of Croagh Patrick, Clew Bay, Clare Island and the mountains of Achill. From the Newport-Mallaranny road (N59) turn right up a track at 923 963 and park near a derelict house with a red tin roof in amongst a clump of trees.

Walk a short distance up the track to Glendahurk Bridge and, taking the southern bank of the river, pick the driest route to the gently sloping ridge leading to Ben Gorm (583m/1,912ft). To the south, Clew Bay with its profusion of islands provides a contrasting foreground for the sharp cone of Croagh Patrick, silhouetted by the midday sun. Lough Feeagh and Furnace Lough are fed by the Srahmore River which in turn is fed by the Altaconey River which springs from the foothills of Nephin Beg rising before you to the north and now girded by forestry plantations.

Descend to the col, noting the transformation of the bog to your left by forestry developments, and then climb the main ridge to the rocky summit of Corrannabinnia 714m/2,343ft. The western prospect is bog, and more bog, stretching to the sea.

The energetic may like to continue to Glennamong (*Gleann an mong*, Sedge Glen: 630m/2,067ft) along the cliff-lined ridge overlooking Corrannabinnia and Corryloughaphuill Loughs. Otherwise, take the straightforward descent route along the main southward ridge over 438m/1,437ft, picking up the track amongst turf workings several hundred metres above base.

Distance excluding Glennamong: 13km/8miles. Ascent: 840m/2,800ft approx. Walking time: 5½ hours.

Distance including Glennamong: 19.5km/12miles. Ascent: 1,250m/4,100ft.

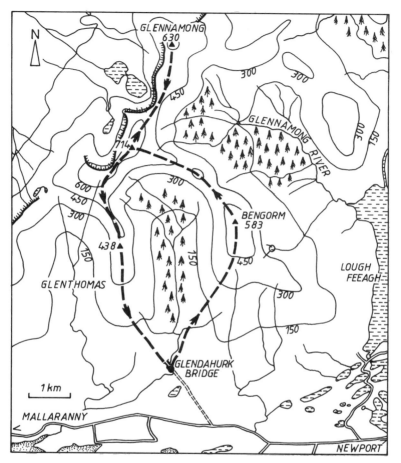

Reference OS Maps: Sheets 30 and 31 (1:50,000).

31. CROAGHMORE-CLARE ISLAND

Clare Island, at the mouth of Clew Bay, is one of the few western islands to offer any hill walking. It is rugged, windswept and isolated but can be reached by regular sailings, when weather and sea conditions permit, from Roonagh Quay, 7km/4.5 miles west of Louisburgh. There are now hotel, guest house, hostel and restaurant facilities for the visitor on the island and taxis, too!

The hill nearest to the harbour, Knocknaveen (222m/729ft) offers some pleasant walking and good views of the island and nearby mainland. However, the seasoned walker will want to climb Croaghmore (sometimes called Knockmore), the hill which gives Clare Island its characteristic profile when viewed from the mainland. It can be reached on foot (or by other means) along the south shore road, passing the sixteenth-century Cistercian Abbey (which in fact is really only a small church) on the way. Follow the road via Toormore to its termination amongst the turf cuttings and then walk up to the signal tower from where you will be able to appraise the walk to come and enjoy the views of the mainland mountains to the east.

Follow the cliff edge as it rises steeply towards the spectacular, steep-sided inlet which punctuates the hillside. Fulmars, sitting on ledges near the bottom of the cliff, will give you an idea of its scale. Take care on the steep slopes, especially when they are wet. You can continue to follow the cliff line or take to the ridge and head for the summit via the trig. point. I prefer the cliff-top route from where I can, in spring and summer, get a glimpse of gannets (*Sula bassana*) nesting on a stack just to the east of the inlet. The gannets colonised the island in the 1970s but only two or three pairs have bred each year so far. Choughs are numerous along the cliff and with luck peregrines can be seen, too.

To the northwest the cliffs of Achill Head project saw-like into the Atlantic and further east, as you reach the high point of the cliffs, the Nephins unfold and direct your eyes inland and southwards to the island-studded inner reaches of Clew Bay and the majestic cone of Croagh Patrick.

The descent is steep and slippery, even in dry conditions, the sward being grazed to billiard-table smoothness by an excess of sheep and rabbits. A glance to the seaward side of the fence illustrates dramatically the difference between ungrazed and grazed vegetation. Inland, the hill slopes and moorland are equally bared, the rich vegetation of a century ago seriously diminished.

Down in the bogs, with their relict pine stumps, new discoveries are being made of ancient cooking places (*fulachta fiadh*) and Neolithic habitations and tombs. Man has occupied Clare Island, perhaps continually, for five thousand years or more. In fact, the island is steeped in history. It was, for example, the stronghold of the legendary pirate queen Granuaile (Grace O'Malley) in the sixteenth century and, in the early part of the twentieth century, the subject of the Clare Island Survey — a uniquely comprehensive study of the natural and human history of the island organised by Robert Lloyd Praeger.

Follow the undulating ground along the low cliffs to the lighthouse and pick up the road which takes you back to the harbour.

Distance: Toormore to Harbour, 9.7km/6miles. Ascent: 480m/1,600ft. Walking time: 3½ hours.

Distance: full circuit, 16km/10miles. Ascent: 480m/1,600ft. Walking time: 5½ hours.

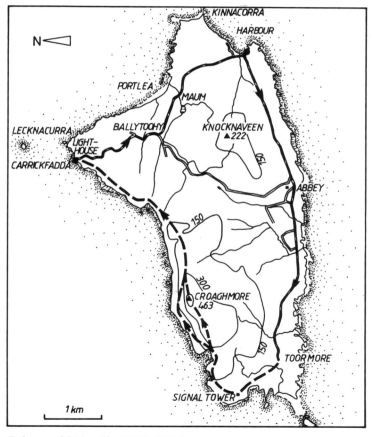

Reference OS Map: Sheet 30 (1:50,000).

32. SLIEVEMORE

Slievemore (672m/2,204ft) is the highest hill on Achill and, like Croaghaun (Cruachan, Round Hill), was once the hunting ground of the eagle (Aquila), after which the island was named (Achaill). But, alas, the hills have not been graced by this majestic bird since the early years of this century.

Approach Slievemore from Doogort (*Dubh gort*, Black Field or *Dumha Goirt*) strand (670 090) taking the road westwards past the last bungalow. Climb the hill, keeping to the left of the crags (which offer some easy climbing). The hill steepens into a sharp ridge which drops away steeply into the corrie on your right. To the left, the hill slopes gently towards Keel Lough. The views from the summit, like those from Croaghaun, are magnificent and all embracing. In particular, there is an excellent view of Blacksod Bay, the Mullet and the low-lying Inishkea Islands. The latter are now uninhabited, but in the winter they provide a safe home for over half of Ireland's barnacle geese (*Branta leucopsis*).

From the summit descend westward to the plateau, taking in the deep cleft in the mountainside to the north if you wish, and then turn south towards the deserted village at the foot of the hill (640 075). To the west of the village there is a quartz quarry beside the track leading over to Dooagh. At the village take the track eastwards to the graveyard, turn right and then left and you're on the road back to Doogort. Anyone interested in examining the cromlech on the southern slope is advised to locate it on a compass bearing from the summit or some other suitable reference point, because otherwise it is difficult to find.

Distance: 9.7km/6miles. Ascent: 670m/2,200ft. Walking time: 4 hours.

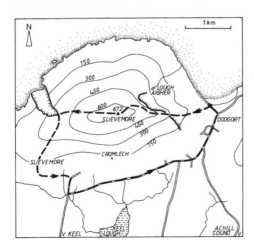

Reference OS Map: Sheet 30 (1:50,000).

33. CROAGHAUN

Croaghaun (Cruachan, Round Hill: 668m/ 2,192ft) is the most westerly hill in the region and also the site of some of the most spectacular cliffs in the country, which plunge steeply to the sea almost from the summit cairn. Unfortunately, they can only be viewed properly from the sea or from the knife-edge ridge which forms Achill Head.

The best walk, taking in Croaghaun, starts at the secluded strand at Keem Bay (560 045). Climb up the grassy slope to the south towards the derelict Marconi signal tower atop Moyteoge Head. Follow the ridge westwards, taking in two steep benches and keeping a wary eye on the precipitous gullies which offer unrestricted passage to the sea for those who make a careless move.

From the high point on Benmore descend to the boggy valley which leads you on to the steep craggy and broken slopes of Croaghaun. A detour via Achill Head should satisfy those with surplus adrenalin. The summit cairn is soon reached and from it you can see the mountains and islands of Connemara in the south, the cliff tops of the north Mayo coast and all prominent stations in between. Continue along the cliff top nearly to Lough Bunnafreeva West, perched right on the edge of the cliff. Then turn southeast to the rim of the large, sharply ribbed corrie which dramatically cradles Lough Acorrymore, (*Loch an corrie mor*, Lough of the Big Corrie). This now serves as a reservoir and the road serving it takes you easily and quickly back to the coast road and your starting point. Alternatively, you can cut off the corner by crossing the hill and joining the coast road nearer to Keem Strand.

Distance: 11.3km/7miles. Ascent: 750m/2,500ft approx. Walking time: 5 hours.

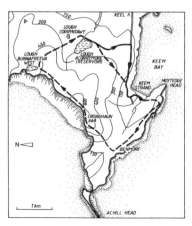

Reference OS Map: Sheet 30 (1:50,000).

34. NORTH MAYO CLIFFS

The walk from the small fishing village of Porturlin to Belderg Harbour offers some of the most spectacular coast walking in the west of Ireland. Contorted Precambrian metamorphic rocks rise steeply from the sea, at some points to a height of about 300m/ 1,000ft.

To avoid difficulties reaching the cliff from the harbour start from the track to the southeast (890 418) and head directly across the bog to the cliff top. From here you have magnificent, contrasting views which will enchant you throughout the walk. Looking north-eastwards across the open sea you can see Donegal and the great cliffs of Slieve League and to the north-west the almost pyramidal Stags of Broadhaven in their glorious isolation. Inland the vastness of the north Mayo bogs is breathtaking. Only the scattering of cottages and new forestry plantations give scale to this unique landscape.

The walking is reasonably easy but steep in places, a mixture of grass and sedge sward and low heather with some peat hagging on the higher ground.

Seabird life on the cliffs is sparse, fulmars being the main occupants of the cliff ledges in summer. But peregrines also frequent the cliffs — where sea eagles once bred. Diminutive, dowdy and uncommon twites (*Carduelis [Acanthis] flavirostris*) breed on the cliff-top slopes.

Forestry plantations, many of their trees browned by the salt air, are filling up the low ground below Skelp and here they are swallowing up old cottages, surely some of the remotest dwellings even in this sparsely populated area.

Beyond Skelp the cliff turns northwards into a promontory below which you can see the whale-backed island of Illanmaster, a bird sanctuary and the home of many thousands of storm petrels and puffins which nest in burrows on the grassy slopes. Then, after a steep descent you take the broad sweep up to Glinsk, the high point of the walk. The descent takes you to Moista Sound, a spectacular gash in the cliff where a softer igneous dyke has succumbed to the forces of the sea. From here you can follow **the** long stretch of bog down to Belderg, bypassing Benwee Geevraun Point on the way. Ahead you can see the lowlands of Ballycastle with Doonbristy, a now isolated stack defiantly standing alone at the point of Downpatrick Head.

In Belderg you should visit the excavated remains of Neolithic and Bronze Age farms and, if you have time, the Ceide Fields at Behy, about 6.5km/4miles east on the road to Ballycastle. From the Interpretative Centre on the cliff edge, you overlook 1,000 hectares of prehistoric walled fields overlain by peatbog, which have been either excavated or located by sounding through the peat. It is difficult to imagine that this area was more heavily populated with farming people five thousand years ago than it is today!

Distance: Porturlin-Belderg, 11.3km/7miles. Ascent: 600m/2,000ft.
Walking time: 4½ hours.

Distance: Including return to Porturlin by the track, 22.6km/14miles.
Ascent: 600m/2,000ft. Walking time: 7 hours.

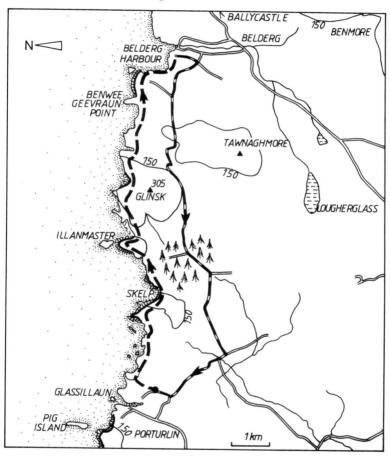

Reference OS Map: Sheet 23 (1:50,000).

INTRODUCTION

The walks described start in south Sligo and are numbered northwards. As the experienced walker will find countless variations for each walk, there is no need to stick rigidly to the routes which have been set out. A good bump of locality counts for much of the walk's enjoyment. The times suggested are those that would be taken by an averagely fit adult but excluding some time for resting and admiring the landscape. If you intend to deviate from the marked route, you should adjust your time and distance calculations accordingly. Where a particular walk finishes some miles from the starting point, it is assumed that the single walker or a group will have previously left some form of transport at the finishing point, prior to the start of the walk, if they wish to avoid a return road walk. Alternatively, a larger group with several vehicles available can split into two parties — each starting from the opposite end, and exchanging car keys half way.

The route maps have been much improved over the previous edition, and new 1:50,000 OS maps cover the northwest on thirteen sheets.

We are still fortunate that in the 1990s there is little restraint placed on walkers in our hill regions in Ireland. This is not the case in some other countries, and the increasing number of overseas visitors who come to these shores every year probably appreciate this freedom more than we do. It is imperative therefore that land owners' rights are respected, if walkers are to maintain the existing good relations. Care should be taken to close all gates, as well as in crossing fences, so as to cause no damage or strain on the wires. Stones inadvertently dislodged from walls should be replaced. All cans, paper and plastic bags should be returned to your rucksack and not deposited around the hills or on the summit cairns. The motto of the countryside ought to read — take only pictures, leave only footprints. A further note of advice regards dogs. If they must be taken, they should be kept on a lead, particularly during the lambing season.

Since the last guide, continued ramblings on the hills of the northwest and further afield with numerous friends has provided me with many days of pleasant company through all types of weather. In particular I would like to thank Stephen Birkett for providing material on the flora and to Gerry and Kathleen Foley for hospitality and advice during visits to Sligo last summer. Thanks also to Joss Lynam for conducting me through the preparation for this new guide.

Access and Accommodation

Access to the northwest from mainland Britain is by Stena Line and P&O routes to Larne (Co. Antrim) from Cairnryan and Stranraer. The nearest airports are Belfast International and Belfast Harbour. Other small regional airports which may be of use are at Eglinton near Londonderry, Carrickfin near Bunbeg (West Donegal) and Sligo Regional Airport (Strandhill).

Daily express buses operate from Dublin to Donegal. One route travels via Enniskillen to Donegal Town, and the other to Letterkenny via Monaghan, Omagh and Lifford. Sligo is served by rail from Dublin, as well as an express bus linking southern towns. Londonderry is served by rail from Belfast as well as express bus via Dungannon and Strabane.

From Londonderry and Strabane there are connecting links both to the Lough Swilly Omnibus Service, serving Inishowen and north Donegal and to the Bus Eireann bus network serving south Donegal, Leitrim and Sligo. There are weekend express buses in July and August from Glasgow (via Stranraer) to three centres in Donegal — Carndonagh (Inishowen), Letterkenny and Bundoran. In addition, a number of private bus companies run buses between west Donegal and Scotland. Most towns in the county are connected with Dublin by McGeehan's, a private bus service that runs to Dublin every morning and returns every evening (including Sundays).

The hills of Inishowen can be explored using local bus routes which link the various towns and villages. The peninsulas of Fanad and Rosguill are served by bus from Letterkenny. A route south of Letterkenny travels to Gartan on the shore of Lough Gartan, with its forest park and the mountains surrounding the adjacent Glenveagh National Park. From Londonderry twice-daily services (except Sundays) travel to Letterkenny and Dunglow (*An Clochan Liath*), giving access to the Muckish-Errigal range. There are youth hostels in this area at Arranmore Island (683 156) accessible by ferry from Burtonport; Crohy Head (710 073), 8km/5miles southwest of Dunglow and at Dunlewy (908 201).

South Donegal is served by bus from Londonderry, via Ballybofey to Donegal town and hence south to Bundoran and Sligo, passing the Dartry Mountains en route. West of Donegal Town, a route travels west to Glencolumbkille via Killybegs and Carrick. From Ballybofey a route travels to Glenties via Fintown, terminating on the scenic Dawros peninsula at Portnoo.

A bus route travels from Sligo, through the limestone scenery via Manorhamilton to Blacklion, convenient to the Tiltinbane-Cuilcagh Mountains and continues to Enniskillen, centre for the Fermanagh lake district, the Marble Arch Caves and the Florencecourt Forest Park. Southwest of Sligo, a route travels to Charlestown via Aclare, near the Ox Mountains.

While these routes should not alter to any great extent, the times will vary between summer and winter schedules. It is advisable to check with the appropriate transport company before you finalise travel arrangements.

The cheapest accommodation is provided by the modest facilities of the

Irish Youth Hostels Association (An Oige). There are five of these in Donegal and a franchised one in Sligo town but none in Leitrim or Cavan. Further information can be obtained from An Oige, 61 Mountjoy Street, Dublin 1 (Tel. 01-8304555, Fax 01-8305808). The Youth Hostels Association of Northern Ireland have hostels at Castle Archdale Country Park, 18km/11miles north of Enniskillen on the shore of Lower Lough Erne, and a temporary one (at the time of writing) in Londonderry. In addition there are thirteen independent hostels throughout the area listed in the *Independent Hostel Owners Guide*. Two are in Co. Sligo and eleven in Co. Donegal. There is also accommodation at the Malinmore Adventure Centre near Glencolumbkille.

A variety of accommodation is provided throughout the area by hotels, guest houses and farm houses. A plentiful supply of bed and breakfast accommodation exists, especially along the coastal routes. Travellers can readily obtain up-to-date holiday information leaflets from the local tourist offices throughout the northwest, or from the headquarters of the North Western Regional Tourism Organisation, Temple Street, Sligo (Tel. 071-61201).

Self-catering, Irish-style cottages are available for renting at a number of locations, including Glencolumbkille, Malinmore and Cruit Island (near Dunglow). There are also organised camping and caravan sites situated mainly at small resorts on the coast. These are located at Ballymastocker Bay and at Rockhill in Fanad, Downings and Marble Hill on Sheep Haven, Narin on Gweebarra Bay and at Fintragh near Killybegs.

Similar facilities exist further south at Bundoran, Mullaghmore and Strandhill west of Sligo. The Fermanagh lake district has camping and caravan facilities at Castle Archdale, Kesh, on the Colebrooke River near Lisnaskea and at Lough Navar and Monea on the south side of the Lower Lough. There are also chalets at Ely Lodge in a woodland setting on the Lower Lough. Further west at Lough Melvin there is the Lough Melvin Holiday Centre.

Camping and caravanning facilities exist in Co. Tyrone at Drum Manor near Cookstown, Parkanaur near Castlecaulfield, the Gortin Glen Caravan and Camping park near Omagh, and at Fivemiletown and Newtownstewart. In Co. Derry, facilities exist at Ballyronan, Castlerock, Downhill, Loughermore Forest (near Claudy), Coleraine, Limavady, the Roe Valley Country Park and at Portstewart.

Elsewhere if the independent camper takes a little trouble to seek permission to camp on what looks like private ground, short term camping is hardly ever refused. Obviously the site should be left as clean as when you found it. Whether you travel by car or by the more leisurely pedal cycle, walkers and explorers will discover that there are a maze of minor roads and tracks (not shown on the small-scale tourist maps) leading into the remotest hill areas. Many of those roads have been upgraded over the last two decades. Unlike the Scottish Highlands, where large tracts are far removed from access roads, the position in Ireland is different. It is probably true to say that all the hill summits in the northwest lie no more than two miles from an access road.

Geology

The topography of the northwest provides as rich a variety of geology, scenery and walking terrain as any other part of the country. The vertical cliff-girt limestone plateaux of Sligo and Leitrim contrast strongly with the subdued Ox Mountains further west and the granites and quartzites in Donegal. Both the ancient rocks of the Pre-Cambrian Era, together with the newer sedimentary layers of the Palaeozoic Era are displayed.

The broad geological history of the area centres around three main periods. Firstly, Pre-Cambrian which ended some 600 million years ago, when virtually no known life existed. This period saw the birth of the oldest rocks in Ireland, representing the tail-end of the Caledonian mountain building system. Much of the original rock has since been eroded, and it is now the mere roots of this system which forms the highest summits in the northwest.

Secondly, the Palaeozoic Era which lasted over 350 million years, and is represented by the granites of Donegal and the massive limestones of the Sligo-Fermanagh area. Thirdly, the relatively recent Pleistocene epoch, when the Great Ice Age was responsible for the final moulding of the present-day landscape.

In Donegal the most geologically complex of all the Irish counties, the Pre-Cambrian rocks exhibit a marked northeast to southwest trend. The most distinctive feature of this 'graininess' is exemplified by the Glenveagh-Gweebarra tear fault valley. Numerous other faults picked out by fluvial and glacial erosion profoundly influence the topography. Here, the three dominant rock types are the quartzites, schists, and gneisses, which have all been highly metamorphosed. These rocks which occupy the greater part of the area, have been found by radioactive methods of dating to be more than 500 million years old. As well as embracing most of Donegal, they are distributed widely throughout Tyrone and west Londonderry. In these areas the intractable quartzites which form the highest summits are missing, thus giving more subdued hill topography.

The Palaeozoic era which followed the Pre-Cambrian is represented mainly in the Sligo-Fermanagh region where it produced the extensive limestone, the youngest rocks in the northwest. These landscapes are dominated by vast sheets of limestone of the Carboniferous age, whose surface features and underground caves are a tribute to the solutional power of rainwater. The plateaux are cut into by wide grikes and hollows (dolines). The subsequent blanket bog which has developed over the last 4,000 years means that many of these hollows are bridged by peat. Further north however, there were massive intrusions of granite into the existing rocks of Donegal. The largest of these intrusions, covering 224sq.km/140sq.miles builds the Derryveagh and Glendowan Mountains, on either side of the Gweebarra fault valley. Another older granite area on the west coast called the Rosses has been greatly reduced by erosion to an irregular plateau of about 60m/200ft. Several phases of granite intrusion form the Blue Stacks, which rise to over 600m/2,000ft, north of Donegal Bay, as well as the Barnesmore Hills.

In the east, an escarpment of tertiary basalt overlooks the Foyle lowlands in north Co. Londonderry at Binevenagh, while further south, the subdued schist uplands of the Sperrins lack the quartzite drama of neighbouring Donegal. In the southeast the landscapes of south Fermanagh and central Cavan are characterised by a drumlin topography of low hills overlying the Palaeozoic rocks and interspersed by badly drained lowlands, a confused drainage system and numerous small lakes.

The third and final period was the Great Ice Age of the Pleistocene epoch which ended about 10,000 years ago. All the effects of severe glaciation can be seen throughout the northwest. The ice eroded surfaces and U-shaped valleys are most evident in Donegal. The Derryveagh Mountains were a major centre of local glaciation, where ice moving mainly north and northwest carved out the Poisoned Glen and modified the trough of Glenveagh. During the maximum phase of the glaciers, countless numbers of granite boulders were carried far from their original source. One of these enormous rocks can be seen, perched beside the road just south of Crolly in the Rosses area. Deep glacial breaches have considerably lowered the Muckish-Errigal ridge, such as at Muckish Gap and at Altan Lough. Further south, the Blue Stacks also acted as an ice centre, and display features of glacial erosion such as rock grooving, truncated valley spurs, erratic boulders and the cirque containing Lough Belshade. The work of the ice can easily be appreciated in Barnesmore Gap where polished granite walls indicate that the pre-glacial spurs have been completely obliterated by ice moving northeast from the Lough Eske area. Some of the higher summits such as Errigal may have stood above the ice sheets as nunataks. Glacial deposition, resulting in low regular hills called drumlins are the main feature in Co. Cavan, as well as around the head of Donegal Bay.

Immediately south of the main Sperrins ridge, the scenic Glenelly valley was formerly the site of one of the larger ice damned lakes in the area which later found an outlet or 'spillway' at Barnes Gap.

In the Sligo-Leitrim area, retreating ice in many of the valleys has caused the over-steepened sides to break away in huge blocks, as seen for example in the picturesque Swiss Valley in Glencar, and at the sinister Eagle's Rock in Glenade.

Flora and Fauna

Flora   The plant, animal and bird life of the region is dictated to a large extent by the geology and climate, which together have created a variety of habitats. The high hills and ridges support little in the way of resident plants and animals, and it is only on the lower slopes, boglands, pastures and lakes, that a diversity of species becomes apparent. In contrast to the hard crystalline rocks of the Donegal Highlands, the lime-rich soils of Sligo and parts of Leitrim support a much richer flora. In this brief summary, the Latin names for the more common plants and animals are included, to aid visitors from abroad.

The lower moorlands throughout the northwest support the ubiquitous gorse/furze/whin (*Ulex*) which is a blaze of fragrant yellow bloom in early summer. Bracken (*Pteridium aquilinum*) often grows in association with the gorse on better drained sheltered places. Most spectacular are the fuchsias (*Fuchsia magellanica*) a native of Chile which inhabit the relatively frost-free valleys of the west coast, where its profuse hedges are aflame with red flowers in late summer.

The limestone areas of Sligo and Leitrim support an exceptionally rich flora, particularly the alpine and calcicole plants, which inhabit the sides and gullies of the limestone plateaux between Lough Gill and Lough Melvin. These include the mountain sorrel (*Oxyria digyna*), purple saxifrage (*Saxifraga oppostifolia*), dwarf mountain or least willow (*Salix herbacea*), holly fern (*Polystichum lonchitis*), alpine meadow rue (*Thalictrum alpinum*), mountain avens (*Dryas octopetala*) and the delicate maidenhair-fern (*Adiantum capillus-veneria*). The high cliffs such as on Benbulbin harbour the more interesting of the most inaccessible species such as the only Irish stations of the alpine saxifrage (*Saxifraga nivalis*) and chickweed willow-herb (*Epilobium alsinifolium*). Here too is the only station in the British Isles of the fringed sandwort (*Arenaria ciliata*).

The acid nutrient-deficient soils of Donegal are a complete contrast. Here, where the land is washed on three sides by the Atlantic and with accompanying harsh wet winds, many alpine-arctic plants have been forced to descend to lower altitudes than elsewhere in the country. These include the hoary whitlow grass (*Draba incana*), purple saxifrage, alpine meadow-rue, and alpine saw-wort (*Saussurea alpina*). The Atlantic's warming influence has also allowed plants such as the Killarney fern (*Trichomanes speciusum*) and the maidenhair fern to flourish outside their southwestern habitat. Donegal boasts certain North American rarities, such as pipe-wort (*Eriocaulon septangulare*) and the slender naiad (*Najas flexilis*), which grow in the shallow bog lakes as well as water lobelia (*Lobelia dortmanna*) and blue-eyed grass (*Sisyrinchium bermudiana*). While the north face of Slieve League above Lough Agh supports some of the alpine-arctic flora mentioned, there are interesting non-alpine plants such as several uncommon hawkweeds (*Hieracium*) on the rich swards of the mountain.

On lower ground and in the glens one finds holly (*Ilex aquifolium*), rowan or mountain ash (*Sorbis aucupana*), juniper (*Juniperus communis*), a variety of mosses and liverworts and the insectivorous butterworts (*Pinguicula spp.*) as well as several varieties of orchids (*Dactylorhiza sp.*).

The main Lusitanian representative is the St Patrick's cabbage (*Saxifraga spathularis*) which resembles London Pride. It can be found growing among the rocks up to quite high levels, as for example on Muckish. The casual visitor to the mountains will notice the vast tracts of common ling (*Calluna vulgaria*) interspersed with bell heather (*Erica cinerea*), and in damper places, crossleaved heath (*Erica tetralix*) and rushes (*Juncus*). Bilberry/ blaeberry/whortleberry (*Vaccinum myrtillus*) and crowberry (*Empetrum nigrum*) are also abundant.

Further to the east in Derry and Tyrone the more fertile basaltic soils of the Binevenagh escarpment support mountain avens, saxifrages and other alpines. The more hospitable schists of the Sperrins support a continuous carpet of vegetation to over 600m/2,000ft providing a habitat to the usual alpines already mentioned.

The climax woodland that colonised the northwest when the climate ameliorated after the ice-age was composed of willow, birch, hazel, pine, alder, oak, elm and ash. Fragmentary stands of these still exist in Glenveagh, Lough Eske, Lough Gill and other small areas.

Fauna The variety of fauna on the northern hills is relatively limited, and apart from the Irish Red Deer (*Cervus elephas*) little is known about the animal communities that occupy the various upland habitats. Some of the commoner birds encountered in open country include the curlew (*Numenius arquata*), meadow pipit (*Anthus pratensis*), skylark (*Alauda arvensis*), stonechat (*Saxicola torquata*) and the wheatear (*Oenanthe oenanthe*), a summer visitor. The common sandpiper (*Tringa hypoleucos*) frequents the shores of the moorland lakes in summer, while in winter, flocks of snow buntings (*Plectrophenax nivalis*) can be observed on the high ground. The red grouse (*Lagopus lagopus*) which breeds on the heather hillsides has an evocative flight call. It is occasionally seen, though it is becoming scarce. So also is the secretive summer visitor, the corncrake (*Crex crex*) which still manages to nest in the hayfields in the Dunfanaghy and Falcarragh areas of north Donegal as well as the Fanad peninsula.

The more frequent birds of prey include the peregrine falcon (*Falco peregrinus*) which is an endangered species, though the hovering kestrel (*Falco tinnunculus*) is a more familiar sight. The sparrow hawk (*Accipiter nisus*) is more often encountered in wooded areas, as well as the largest raptor, the buzzard (*Buteo buteo*). The common crow (*Corvus corone cornix*) is an adaptable and useful scavenger, while the raven (*Corvus corax*) is often seen, circling over the mountain cliffs. The majestic golden eagle (*Aquila chrysaetos*) which formerly bred in such places as Glenveagh and the Poisoned Glen up to the turn of the century, is no longer with us.

The great sea cliffs such as at Horn Head and Slieve League in Donegal provide nesting sites for choughs (*Pyrrhocorax pyrrhocorax*), fulmars (*Fulmaris glacialis*), guillemots (*Uria aalgae*), kittiwakes (*Rissa tridactyle*), puffins (*Fratercula arctica*) and razorbills (*Alca torda*). The off-shore islands are the breeding ground for eider duck (*Somateria molissima*).

The lakes are the habitat for a variety of the duck family such as the ubiquitous little grebe or dabchick (*Podiceps ruficollis*), the tufted duck (*Aythya fuligula*) and the teal (*Anas crecca*). The grey heron (*Ardea cinera*) can also be seen, patiently waiting for prey at both river and lake edge. The smallest of the divers, the red-throated (*Gavia stellata*) is known to breed in Donegal in small lakes within flying distance of the sea.

Looking briefly at wildfowl, the Greenland white-fronted goose (*Anser albifrons flavirostris*), the whooper swan (*Cygnus cygnus*) and the barnacle goose (*Branta leucopsis*) winter at Lissadell and Mullaghmore in Sligo. The graceful mute swan (*Cygnus obor*) is widely distributed on the larger lakes. Other places for observing wildfowl include the flats adjacent to Inch Island in Lough Swilly, Trawbreaga Bay in Inishowen, Mulroy Bay, the New Lake sanctuary at Dunfanaghy and Sheskinmore Lough Reserve near Rosbeg which also supports many varieties of orchid.

The largest mammal found in the mountainous areas is the Irish Red Deer. The Glenveagh National Park has one of the finest herds in Ireland. A considerable number of fallow deer (*Dama dama*) inhabit the woodlands around Slieve Dacane and Slish Wood in Sligo, and were reputed to have been introduced by the Normans in the thirteenth century. Several hundred Sika deer (*Cervus nippon*) inhabit the Baronscourt Estate in Co. Tyrone. Herds of feral goats (*Capra sp.*) roam the Ox Mountains and Knockalla in north Donegal.

The common or red fox (*Vulpes vulpes*) is widespread, but like the badger (*Meles meles*) is rarely seen in daylight. The Irish hare (*Lepus timidus*) is fairly widely distributed and can be observed up to quite high levels. The rabbit (*Oryctolagus cuniculus*) population has recovered substantially since the 1950s devastation by the myxomatosis virus. The shy red squirrel (*Sciurus vulgaria*) frequents the woodlands around Lough Gill. The elusive Irish stoat (*Mustela erminea hibernica*) can occasionally be glimpsed. It should not be confused with some of the mink that have escaped from commercial mink farms in west Donegal. Little is known about the rare pine marten (*Martes martes*) in the northwest, but it is likely that the new conifer forests will improve its chance of survival.

History and Archaeology

There has been human settlement in the northwest since the Irish Mesolithic period (around 7000 BC) and many varieties of prehistoric tombs remain, especially from the Neolithic and Early Bronze Age (4000 BC). St Patrick brought Christianity to the area and his name is long associated with Lough Derg in Donegal. St Columcille (Columba), who was born at

Gartan in north Donegal in AD 521, established a settlement on Iona off the Scottish coast.

Later settlers such as the Vikings and Normans made less impression in this region than in the south and east of the country. The hill margins were the favoured habitats of the first farmers who had penetrated into most parts of the island by the beginning of the second millennium BC. Down through the centuries the hills came to serve as territorial bases for local clans and patriotisms. The plantation of west Ulster by English and Scottish colonists in the early part of the seventeenth century followed the event known as 'the flight of the Earls', when the Earls of Tyrone and Tyrconnell (Donegal) fled with a company of friends and retainers to France in 1607.

In Sligo, an area rich in mythic tales and prehistoric sites, tombs erected by Neolithic farmers some 5,000 years ago were well seen on the ridges of Carrowkeel in the south of the county. The great cairn on the isolated hill of Knocknarea is supposedly the grave of Queen Maeve of Connaught. Close by, a series of tombs and a passage grave sited on natural mounds can be seen at Carrowmore, the largest Megalithic cemetery in Europe. Drumcliff High Cross and the stump of a round tower — the remains of a monastic establishment founded by St Columba — are convenient to W. B. Yeats's grave on the N15 north of Sligo. Further north there is an extensive court-tomb at Creevykeel near Cliffony.

In Co. Cavan, another court-tomb built around 3000 BC exists at Cohair to the southeast of Cootehill. Cloghoughter is an early example of a round castle which occupies a rock island in Lough Oughter. Seized by the Cromwellians in 1653 it has been in ruins ever since.

In north Donegal in the Inishowen peninsula, the Carndonagh Cross, one of the oldest low-relief crosses standing in Ireland has ribbon interlacing similar to the Book of Durrow, with smaller details in a Viking style. Dooey sandhills on Gweebarra Bay was the site of an Early Christian jewellers' workshop, where the site yielded ingots, crucibles, bronze pins and moulds. The Glencolumbkille valley which has been occupied since early Neolithic times, contains an impressive number of decorated slabs and pillars.

There are two fine stone forts in Donegal. The Grianan of Aileach on its hilltop site west of Derry provides the visitor with a wide panorama, while the lesser known Doon Fort occupies a lake island near Narin on the west coast and is accessible by boat. The great portal dolmens at Kilclooney about 2km/1.5miles southeast of the latter is perhaps the finest example in the northwest.

A number of fine castles and abbeys exist throughout the area. Parkes Castle in Leitrim on the shore of Lough Gill featured prominently in the Ulster rebellion of 1641 and has recently been restored as a Visitor Centre. Sligo Abbey was founded as a Dominican priory in 1253. Inishmurray Island in Donegal Bay has a remarkable Early Christian monastery contained within a pear-shaped enclosure. Donegal Castle (fifteenth century) was later remodelled into a Jacobean manor-house by Sir Basil Brooke, an English planter. Also at Donegal Town are the remains of a fifteenth-century Franciscan friary. The sixteenth-century Doe Castle with its impressive central tower stands on the shore of Sheep Haven in north Donegal, while over in Inishowen an Anglo-Norman castle guards the entrance to Lough Foyle at Greencastle.

In the early years of the nineteenth century, a number of watch towers were built on headlands around the coast to guard against a Napoleonic invasion. Many of these are still in a good state of preservation.

Key Map

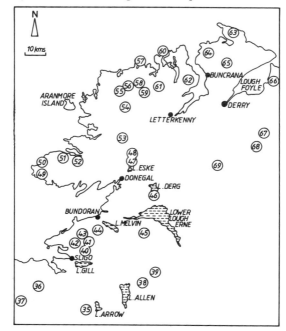

35. BRICKLIEVE (CARROWKEEL) MOUNTAIN

The modest height of Bricklieve or Carrowkeel (An Cheathramha Chaol, Narrow Quarter: 322m/1,057ft) in south Sligo, comprises four parallel limestone ridges, aligned in a NNW-SSE direction and divided by steep-sided dry valleys. The effects of this differential denudation among the various limestone beds is well seen on the approach road (N4) between Sligo and Boyle.

Access to a walk over its interesting terrain, which is also something of an archaeological *tour de force*, is by turning right at Castlebaldwin, and following the signs for 'Carrowkeel Passage Tombs' for 3km/2miles. The road bears left beyond the school and winds uphill, where there is another sign to the left (uphill) just past a small farm in conifers. You should park at the T-junction just over the top of the hill (740 123).

A driveable road runs south up the valley, but the walking route ascends the low right-hand ridge to the clearly visible stone cairn at the summit. A larger one tops the hill on the opposite side. The route opens up views of the dome of Keshcorran (362m/1,188ft) to the northwest, and to the south towards Lough Gara. The cairn or tomb has a passage extending in for about 4m/13ft. This is one of thirteen Bronze Age burial tombs that you can visit on this walk. Some attain heights of 6m/20ft and contain passage ways or cruciform chambers. All were built *c*.2,500 B.C. it is thought, by people of Spanish or Breton origin.

Continue a little south of the cairn, bearing left to descend through a break in the cliffed edge to the valley road. Aim for the steep slope of the central ridge, across a higher road and climb to the large cairn, considered by archaeologists who excavated these sites in 1911 to be the gem of this cemetery. Unfortunately, most of the corbelled roof has collapsed behind the entrance. A little to the north, there is a long cairn which has a fore-court on its south side and a passage grave at the other end. It seems likely from the large stones and slabs used in the building of these structures, that these ridges were at that time quite bare of the present-day peat covering.

Walking east across the central ridge takes you to the head of a short valley, where you ascend to a pair of cairns just north of the summit. One has an intact entrance and a low passage. Further down the ridge, there are two more which can be included on the return walk. The undistinguished summit gives wide views in all directions, particularly north, where between Knocknarea and the Benbulbin plateau country you can spot Slieve League across Donegal Bay. Southwards, you look over the subdued Curlew range and beyond to the midlands.

Two more cairns can be visited to the south of the summit. Proceeding northeast, look for a suitable break in the scarped edge of the two-tiered eastern valley and descend carefully through a fringe of small trees. Make for the wall and fence to the south, which is followed up to a rock face on the opposite side. A scramble up to the left could be classed as a *mauvais pas*, but there is plenty of grass to hold on to. Further up, bear right to the grass-covered unopened cairn.

The entire length of Lough Arrow and its wooded islands is revealed, with Lough Key to the south. Walking north again to the end of this dramatic little ridge takes you past a stone cairn with a tiny partially collapsed entrance. Take care descending off this ridge, as there are short vertical drops. It overlooks a strange area of limestone pavement, reminiscent of the Burren in north Clare, and is the site of a cluster of stone rings or a so-called 'village'.

Walk across this water-sculptured pavement in a northerly direction to the end of the valley, towards a farm in trees. You join a track, through a gate, which you follow up and around the north end of the central ridge. It meets the end of the road at the ancient monument sign, below the two cairns (mentioned earlier). This road curves around the end of the ridge to join the road at the top of the first valley. You can short-cut across to this road which leads downhill through a gate to your starting point.

Distance: 6.4km/4miles. Ascent: 210m/700ft. Walking time: 2¼ hours.

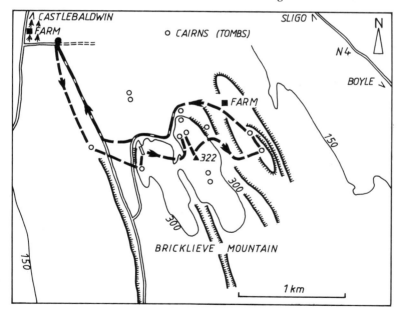

Reference OS Map: Sheet 25 (1:50,000).

36. OX MOUNTAINS-KNOCKALONGY

This rather unfrequented range of hills stretch in a NE to SW line of some 48km/30miles between Collooney in Co. Sligo and Foxford in Co. Mayo. Composed partly of granite, schists and gneisses, they have no connection with oxen, though the Gaelic name of Slieve Ghamh (Stony Mountains) has become confused with Dhamh which would mean Ox Mountains. Separating the Ballina coastal plain from the Central Lowlands and representing an offshoot of the metamorphic rocks of Connemara, they are in marked contrast to the Sligo limestone country. The vertical cliffs and deep glens are entirely absent from these dark heathery and subdued uplands.

Of immediate interest to the hill-walker is the line of small rocky gneiss summits at the eastern end, between Hungry Rock Gap, northeast of Coolaney and the Ladies Brae road. None of these exceeds 370m/1,200ft, but would make an interesting walk in either direction, using return transport. The described walk, however, is to the highest summit of Knockalongy (*Cnoc a Luinge*, Hill of the Encampment: 544m/1,786ft) west of the Ladies Brae.

From Ballisadare, drive west towards Ballina on the N59 for 12.5km/ 7.8miles and turn left just before Skreen at the signpost marked Ladies Brae 5km/3.3miles. The road runs towards the northern slopes of Knocka-chree (*Cnocan a' Chruidhe*, Hill of the Hovel: 538m/1,766ft), ascending gently through maturing conifer plantations to the Brae summit at 244m/800ft. Continue past a T–junction on the left and park where a gated forest track leads off to the right (538 277).

Walk along this track for a little and ascend the hillside on the right, through scattered trees towards the lower slopes of Knockachree. Use the firebreak on the hillside beyond a hollow to clear the top of the plantations. On your left, the whole area surrounding Lough Minnaun and the upper valley of the Owenboy River has been extensively planted. The gradient soon eases and Knockachree's indistinct summit is indicated by a small pile of stones.

The OS pillar on Knockalongy stands 1.6km/1mile southwest like a lone figure on the otherwise featureless plateau. For about half of this dis-tance, you will have to negotiate one of the largest expanses of peat erosion in the northwest, and it can be vilely wet and slippery. As this type of ter-rain really only dries out after a fortnight's drought, progress will normally be energy sapping, until you gain the unbroken grass cover again.

The summit gives a wide panorama in favourable weather. The blunt cone of Nephin backed by the Nephin Beg range across the concealed Lough Conn dominates the west. Northwards, all the landmarks encircling Donegal Bay are visible, from Slieve League right round to the Sligo/Leitrim highlands, with the dome of Knocknarea near Sligo. South-eastwards, the central plain rolls away as a green tapestry towards the River Shannon.

The unmarked and indeterminate top of Knockacappul (*Cnoc an Cappal*, Hill of the Horse: 518m 1,700ft) lies southwest of Knockalongy. It is not sufficiently interesting to visit, unless you wish to extend the walk. With the lack of obvious firebreaks through the plantations surrounding Lough Minnaun limiting a variation in the descent from Knockalongy, it is best to return to the Ladies Brae by the outward route.

Distance: 8km/5miles. Ascent: 300m/1,000ft. Walking time: 2¾ hours.

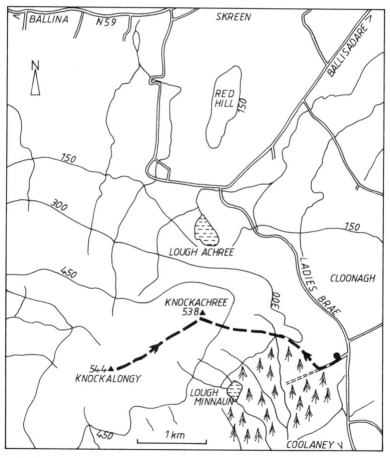

Reference OS Map: Sheet 25 (1:50,000).

37. OX MOUNTAINS: OWENAHER RIVER-EASKY LOUGH

The unclassified road across the Ox Mountains from Dromore West to Mullany's Cross divides the higher eastern tops from those further west in the vicinity of Lough Talt. East of this road, the hills between Easky Lough (Lough an Iascaigh, Lake of the Fish) and the mouth of the Owenaher Valley assume an irregular line. As a bonus, there is little of the broken ground that you encounter on the higher summits further east.

As this is a south to north one-way walk, return transport should be left en route from the Dromore West approach near an abandoned farm at the south end of Easky Lough (450 224). You then drive south for approximately 8km/5miles and start where the hillside and the Owenaher River come closest — there is a wall above the river on the right, with a plantation on the left (443 150). If approaching from the south via the junction of the Coolaney-Mullany's Cross road, the starting point is 1.3km/0.8 miles from this junction.

Your initial ascent alongside the plantation boundary is over bare schist rock and heather and on to the first top at 207m/681ft. You look down on the meandering Owenaher and its small cataract. Now follow a fence on the right for a while, keeping straight on where it turns right. Diverting to the left and slightly downhill, you can look for an erratic boulder on the steep hillside, overlooking a plantation. Although it is locally known as the Rocking or Shaking Stone, I failed to induce any movement from it.

Heading northeast again takes you over the 300m/1,000ft contour, opening up a distant prospect of Easky Lough. Now cross the wide depression, passing to the west of Sussue Common Lake (*Sosadh an Commaun*, the Resting Place of the Little Hollows). The next rise is followed by a descent into a hollow containing the twin Tullyvellia Loughs (*Tulaigh — bheile*, Hill of the Ancient Trees). Crossing the connecting stream, ascend to an unmarked and unnamed summit at 446m/1,465ft.

The highest point on the walk gives views west over the hills surrounding the concealed Lough Talt. Part of Nephin peeps over the western Ox range, but it is the pyramidal sentinel of Croagh Patrick which commands attention in the southwest.

Proceeding north takes you to Glendarragh Lough (*Loch Glen Dara*, Oak Glen Lake). The name is evocative of the oak woods that alas no longer flourish here. Close by, lies Cloonacool Lough South (*Cluin a Cul Loch*, Black Meadow Lake) but you can continue to Cloonacool Lough North.

From here, your descent is to the northwest, following the course of a stream which joins another just before the bridge on the road at Easky Lough and your return transport.

Distance: 8.8km/5.5miles. Ascent: 330m/1,100ft. Walking time: 3 hours.

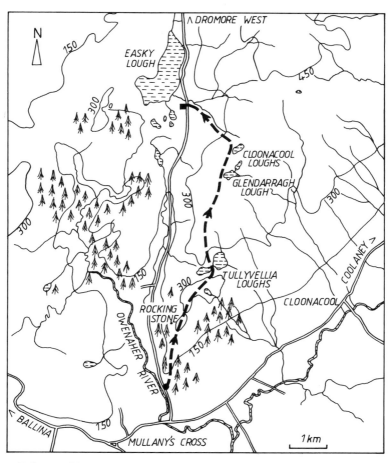

Reference OS Map: Sheet 24 (1:50,000).

38. THE PLAYBANK (SLIEVENAKILLA)

On the borders of Cavan and Leitrim is a range of little known hills, south and west of the Bellavally Gap, which carries the road between Swanlinbar and Dowra. The fairly level terrain, starting south of the Gap, ascends over Point 494m/1,620ft to Benbrack (502m/1,648ft) and then via Corlough Oughter (466m/1,530ft) to skirt Knockgorm Lough and on to the Playbank (542m/1,780ft). This route would make a pleasant day's tramp, without any great ascent or descent. Return transport could be left at Corcashel on the R200, a mile east of Dowra.

The subject of this short walk is the Playbank or Slievenakilla (*Sliab na coille*, Mountain of the Wood). On older maps it is marked as the Playground, so you can take your pick! The origin of the name is obscure, but may be related to a high level summer sports event held in olden times. Its northern escarpment dominates most of the route of the 25km/16miles 'Cavan Way' between Blacklion and Dowra. On the approach road (R207) to Dowra from the Sligo-Enniskillen road (N16) its short plateau has close affinities with its larger neighbour, Cuilcagh to the northeast. A similar crest of sandstone cliffs of Namurian age, is of interest to rock climbers.

Turn left in Dowra and travel for slightly over a 1.7km/1mile along the Glengevlin-Swanlinbar road. Park beside the plantation at Corcashel, or use the driveable road running uphill for 0.8km/0.5miles to a cottage and outbuildings, where there is space for one car at a junction.

Pass through two gates and ascend the green track with a stream on the right and the plantation on the left. Crossing a fence, the ascent over open hillside takes you towards the cliffs on the skyline. There are views over Lough Allen on your right. Deeper heather, mixed with crowberry, surrounds a detached rocky outcrop, below the main cliff, with its pinnacle and wedged boulder.

Avoiding the worst of the jumble of sandstone blocks, keep to the right until you gain the western rim. It is now easy going along the gently rising ridge, with views over the Owenmore River which is fed by the infant Shannon. Soon, the tall cairn appears on the right, which gives wider vistas than the OS pillar about 140m/150yds to the south. Northeastwards, the bulk of Cuilcagh restricts the view, but on the northern horizon you can pick out the Barnesmore Gap hills and the Blue Stacks. Your eye ranges northwest over the back of the Dartry and Benbulbin plateaus, separated by Glenade, with a distant glimpse of Slieve League on the far side of Donegal Bay. Further west, you can discern Queen Maeve's Tomb on top of Knocknarea's bun-like profile near Sligo.

Continue to a slight rise south of the trig. point, and the tapering length of Lough Allen will be revealed, with the featureless swellings of Slieve Anierin (the Iron Mountain) and Bencroy flanking the east shore. Narrow seams of iron ore and coal were once mined from these hills as well as from the Arigna Mountains to the west of the lake. Eastwards, the entire route of the longer walk mentioned is seen, curving round to the Bellavally Gap (335m/1,100ft).

Retracing your steps to the OS pillar, you can return to Corcashel, taking a direct line to the western end of the escarpment, where the descent alongside the stream to the top of the green track leads to the approach road.

Distance: 7.2km/4.5miles. Ascent: 450m/1,500ft. Walking time: 3 hours.

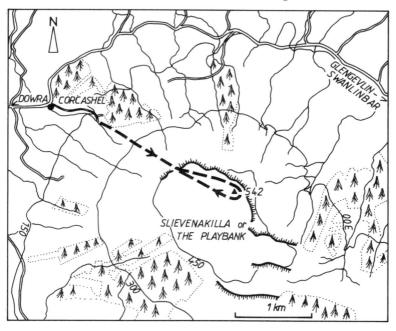

Reference OSNI Map: Sheet 26 (1:50,000).

39. CUILCAGH MOUNTAIN

Cuilcagh (Cailceach, Chalky: 665m/2,188ft) presides benignly over south Fermanagh, sharing the county boundary with Cavan. The long flat-topped ridge (pronounced Kulk-yach) is easily identifiable on the southern skyline on the approaches to Enniskillen, from where it has an implacable presence, 19km/12miles southwest of the town.

The described route is made either from the Sligo direction on the N16 via Blacklion, or from the north, via Enniskillen. Using the latter route, the starting point off the Marlbank Loop road above Claddagh Glen is by turning right at a crossroads off the Enniskillen-Swanlinbar road (A32). Follow the signs for 'Marble Arch Caves' (8km/5miles) past the Florencecourt Demesne and turn left on to the Marlbank road which rises for 3.2 km/2miles, passing the Cave access road on the right. Park a little further on above the wooded depression of the Monastir Sink. This is one of several depressions caused by collapsed limestone caverns. The drainage system from Cuilcagh's northern slopes of Millstone Grit displays karstic characteristics, as the two main rivers gradually disappear underground, down the clefts of Pollawaddy and Pollasumera, on reaching the soluble limestone. They reappear after running through 'caverns measureless to man' as the Claddagh River below the Marble Arch cave system and its underground lake. Part of this hidden underworld, opened to the public in 1985 is now a tourist attraction. The entire area was first explored by a Frenchman, E.A. Martel, in 1897, while Gareth Jones has documented the system in *The Caves of Fermanagh and Cavan*.

To the right of the Monastir Sink, walk over some rushy fields east of a farm track and follow the bank of the Shruh Croppa River. The moorland stretches away towards Tiltinbane (573m/1,881ft). Ground conditions can frequently be wet, making the going somewhat heavy, except after a drought. The obvious bite out of the ridge is the Cuilcagh Gap. Further up, above the junction of the Belbarinagh River which joins the Shruh Croppa on the left, you pass some scant ruins below a fence marking the county boundary. The ground then steepens considerably, and you emerge on to the ridge at the Tiltinbane cairn beside a rocky hollow. The stream rising on the northern slopes of Tiltinbane is the newly discovered source of the River Shannon.

It is easy going for some 4km/2.5miles along the ridge, passing Cuilcagh Gap, where large blocks of sandstone have fallen away. As you move along the crest above Lough Atona, *beware of the fissures in the rock*. The scarp becomes less pronounced as you ascend gradually through heather and large boulders to the main cairn, topped by the OS pillar.

Your panorama on the 'roof' of the Border is more expansive than Tiltinbane, as there is no higher ground between here and the Mourne Mountains. All of the Fermanagh lakeland lies northwards, including Upper Lough Erne and its islands. The conspicuous limestone hills along

Cuilcagh's northern foot are known as 'reef-knolls' and are thought to have been formed from shell banks in the seas of the Carboniferous era. Clear weather reveals all the northwest's familiar landmarks, from Slieve League to Muckish, over 100km/60miles away. Southwards, the scarped edge diminishes towards the Bellavally Gap, which is backed by the Iron Mountains east of Lough Allen and the central plain.

Leaving the cairn, you descend north down the grassy nose. Below a cliffed section are the scant remains of a Cessna aircraft which crashed here in September, 1979. Take a line across the wide moorland towards the Owenbrean River to the west of Skea Hill, beyond which you join a track. This leads through scattered hawthorn trees to a gate on the Marlbank road, a few metres from the Monastir Sink.

Distance: 14.4km/9miles. Ascent: 480m/1,600ft. Walking time: 5 hours.

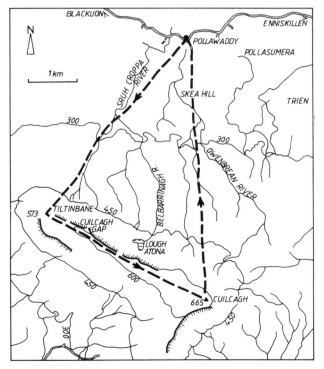

Reference OSNI Map: Sheet 26 (1:50,000).

40. CASTLEGAL MOUNTAIN

The pale grey carboniferous limestones are the youngest rocks in the northwest. Carved into tablelands and dissected by cliff-walled valleys, they brood dramatically over the coastal lowlands of Co. Sligo, where the intricate play of light and shade on the cliffs and aprons of scree, imparts a unique quality of light to the area.

Castlegal, with its fortress-like cliffs, complements the northern scarped edge of Glencar, perhaps the finest of these valleys. The terrain, which has a quartet of tops, is split equally between Sligo and Leitrim. Castlegal (*Caisle Geala*, White Castles: 335m/1,096ft) takes its name from the western top. Crockauns (*Crocaun*, Little Hill: 465m/1,527ft) is the highest point at the east end.

The walk can be done in either direction, with or without return transport. By traversing back along the northern edge in this east-to-west walk, and descending the broad gully opposite the west end of Glencar Lough, you shorten the return road walk.

Starting from the junction of the Glencar and the Sligo-Manorhamilton road (N16) at 780 420 use the gated track a few metres to the left of the N16. It passes a bungalow on the right and continues south through a gate leading to a farm on the left. Ascend through rushy fields towards the lowest point between Crockauns and Hangman's Hill, crossing a small wooded ravine with a ruined house on your right. Climbing up to the left of the forest below the ridge takes you to the upper slopes which are carpeted with primroses in early summer.

The first top gives views eastwards over Hangman's Hill and Keelogyboy. Now follow a ruined wall, going at first downhill and then up along the crest of the cliffs above the forest. Bear left, over green slopes to cross a fence and wall and ascend to the small cairn on Crockauns. Northwards, you look across to the cliffs on the opposite side of Glencar, above which rises Truskmore and the plateau running west to Kings Mountain and Benbulbin Head. Southwards, past the nose of Keelogyboy, lies Lough Gill and the hummocky metamorphic hills culminating in Slieve Daeane.

Your descent to lower heathery ground bypasses a central mound and onwards to the cairnless top of 449m/1,472ft. Further on, the broad gully (mentioned earlier) descends to your right. Continuing west, you pass some limestone knolls to the final grassy summit of Castlegal, where, a little to the west, you have a bird's eye view over the N16.

If return transport is left at this end, it is about half an hour's descent down the left hand ridge to the road, or by using the track that contours across the face of the hillside. Your return along the northern edge, however, yields the most drama on this walk. A rough path threads through the heather above the vertical cliffs. History relates that a certain Sir Frederick Hamilton from Leitrim came to grief here in 1641 after raiding and burning Sligo town. Returning home with his men via

Castlegal, darkness was falling, and a local shepherd was cajoled to guide the raiders over the mountains. The shepherd cunningly led the horsemen to the cliff edge in darkness, instructing them to gallop over a supposedly narrow ditch ahead. In their haste, Hamilton and his band fell to their deaths, and the place has since been known as Hamilton's Leap.

This promenade, high above the mosaic of fields in lower Glencar is a little exposed in places, so *take care*. Around the first bluff, the limestone knolls overlook the plunging cliffs. Contour the hillside, passing a cluster of detached pinnacles, and cross a gully to the next spur. Continue around the spur to cross another gully via a sheep path. An isolated pinnacle can be seen some way down. Keep ascending to the right, around the next spur, until you reach the edge of the broad green gully, with impressive fans of scree beneath the cliffed face on the opposite side.

You descend steeply at first, following the stream to lower ground, and then over some fields to the main road, a short distance to the west of the county boundary. From here, it is about a 45-minute road walk back to the Glencar road junction.

Distance: 9.6 km/6miles. Ascent: 520m/1,700ft. Walking time: 4 hours.

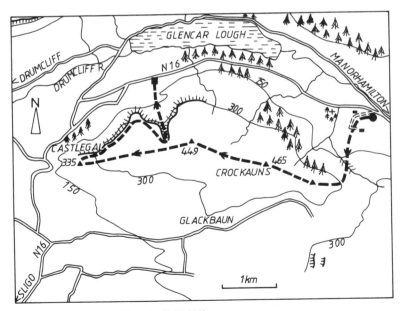

Reference OS Map: Sheet 16 (1:50,000).

41. THE GLENCAR ESCARPMENT

Glencar (Gleann a Chartha, Glen of the Rocks) is the most luxuriantly wooded of all the valleys in the Sligo/Leitrim area. Its northern side has a limestone scarped edge with impressive cliffs running between Kings Mountain and Glencar Waterfall, while the opposite side is overlooked by the rumpled heights of Castlegal.

The walk along the edge uses the more easterly of the two obvious gullies splitting the south face of Kings Mountain. Prior to the start, you can leave return transport or arrange for a lift at the Glencar Waterfall car park, thus avoiding the 4km/2.5miles return road walk.

Approaching from Sligo, follow the signs for Glencar 7.2km/4.5miles, off the N15 at Rathcormack Church. Cross the Drumcliff River to the T–junction, where you turn right and proceed towards Glencar for almost 3.2km/2miles. There is a gate on the left just before Flanagan's shop (on the right), where a field gives access to the foot of the gully.

Climb up the left-hand side under the towering fretted cliff. The gully narrows into a scree chute over a sheep fence. A few metres beyond the fence, the concealed crack of Pinnacle Gully opens on the left. Enter it, and climb over some large blocks, where a short chimney exits to the left. It leads out on to a steep grassy slope which should be ascended *with care* up to and around the head of the main gully. The hard work is now behind you, with gently undulating terrain of grass and knobbly limestone leading eastwards. There are enchanting views down into Glencar and its lake.

After crossing two small valleys, ascend to Tormore (*Tor Mor*, Big Pointed Hill: 388m/1,273ft), the high point of the walk. Truskmore looms to the east and a line of rusting pylons ahead is the remains of an old cable-bucket system. It was used in the extraction of barytes ore from the old workings on your left up the hillside. This soft mineral (barium sulphate), formerly used in the production of paint has found a new use as a lubricant for offshore oil exploration, and is nowadays transported off the mountain by road.

Pass under the pylons towards the cliff edge, where whole sections are seen to have slumped downwards. The locally named 'Swiss Valley' ahead of you below the cliffs has been formed by post-glacial rotational landslips. Descend into a shallow depression and cross a stream where it tumbles over the edge. In strong winds, the water blows backwards in a plume of spray, giving the stream its name of *Struth in Aghaidh an Airdre*, (Stream against the Height).

Keeping to the cliff edge beyond the stream, follow a rough path and cross another stream. You now climb to the sheerest part of the cliffs, above the 'Swiss Valley', where the magnificent precipice high above the mixed woodland is the grand architectural set piece of the walk. There are retrospective views along the escarpment to the lion-like head of Kings

Mountain and out to the coast. The entire length of Castlegal dominates the south.

Continue to keep the edge, through bracken and heather, after which you pass along the top of a conifer plantation to reach an unmade road known as the Bog Road. Cross over the adjacent stream and follow along the forest perimeter to the broad stream feeding the Glencar Waterfall. Pass through a gate on the other side, where a rough path descends through the woods to a right turn on to a green track leading over a bridge. Leave the track about 55m/60yds further on, where it bears right. A path descends on your left through trees and over a fence to an open field.

Follow the trees above the gorge to the bottom left-hand corner of the field to some steps over the fence. Turn left and use the concrete path leading down to the picturesque waterfall. After admiring this elegant cascade plunging over its limestone shelf in the cool leafy glade, continue along the path to the lake-shore car park.

Distance: 7.2km/4.5miles. Ascent: 450m/1,500ft. Walking time: 3 hours.

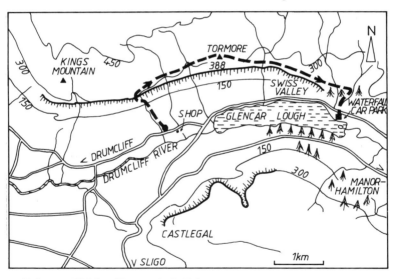

Reference OS Map: Sheet 16 (1:50,000).

42. KINGS MOUNTAIN-BENBULBIN HEAD

Travelling south from Donegal on the N15, the sphinx-like head of Benwhiskin holds your attention beyond Bundoran. Passing Cliffony, the bold scarped edge of Benbulbin (Beann Gulbin, Peak of Gulba) begins to steal the limelight. Further on, in the vicinity of Grange, this famous landmark, immortalised in the poetry of W.B. Yeats, masquerades as a separate mountain, appearing for a few miles to be regally isolated from the main plateau, and making the most of its 527m /1,730ft summit.

This easterly approach from Glendarragh, includes Kings Mountain, a high point on the plateau, south of Benbulbin. Turn left (or right if approaching from Sligo) at Mullaghnaneane crossroads (656 473) signposted Ballaghnatrillick, 8.8km/5.5miles. After 2.2km/1.4miles, turn right at a crossroads and proceed for 3.2km/2miles, passing close under the intimidating walls of the north face, whose fluted buttresses are displayed to perfection by the sun's evening rays. The road goes through conifers and over a bridge. It then climbs alongside the river, where you can park beside or across a small bridge above Ardnaglass Upper at 705 465.

Use the rough track southwards, towards the base of the waterfall descending from the lowest point on the plateau surrounding the spacious embayment between Benwhiskin and Benbulbin. The track peters out, and you bear slightly right, over peat cuttings to ascend either side of the waterfall to gain the plateau. Cross the undulating ground to the top-hatted profile of Kings Mountain (465m/1,527ft), also known as Finn McCool's Table. From the few stones on the summit, you have nice vistas over the scarped southern edge towards Lough Gill and Sligo town, backed by Knocknarea and the distant Ox Mountains.

Now contour the sloping plateau rim to the northwest, around the head of a freshly eroded gully and over a low fence towards the back of Benbulbin Head. Bearing left takes you to the grassy sward on the very edge of the western nose (478m/1,570ft), where the ground plummets dramatically to deciduous and coniferous woodland far below. On a day when a northerly gale battered relentlessly against the cliffs on my right, and huge seas created a white line on the coast, I was able to enjoy a brew-up at this spot in an almost calm vacuum, while absorbing the whole tapestry of the Yeats country beneath my feet.

Keeping as close as possible to the edge of the cliffs and *proceeding with care* will yield sensational views down the most vertical gullies in Ireland. Residual pillars of eroded limestone frame vistas of Benwhiskin's prominent head to the northeast. In early summer you can look for the wide variety of Alpine plants that flourish in the mineral rich soil. This limestone plateau is the only station in the British Isles of the fringed sandwort (*Arenaria ciliata*) and the only Irish station of the alpine saxifrage (*Saxifraga nivalis*). An OS pillar marks Benbulbin's actual summit, south of the eastern nose.

At the end of the north cliffs, turn southeast and continue for a short distance to clear the cliffed edge. You can make an angled descent to Glendarragh and your starting point, via the steep slope with patches of limey shale. Cross the peat cuttings, where a stretch of tarred road leads to the bridge.

Distance: 8.8km/5.5miles. Ascent: 350m/1,150ft. Walking time: 3¼ hours.

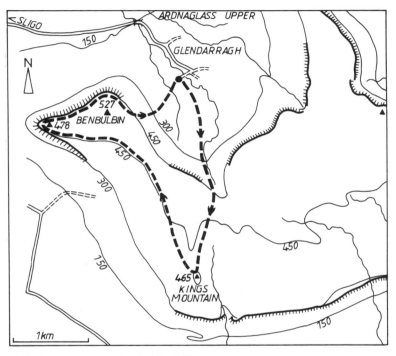

Reference OS Map: Sheet 16 (1:50,000).

43. TRUSKMORE-TIEVEBAUN VIA EAGLES ROCK

Approaching Glenade (Gleann eatha, Glen of Jealousy) on the Manorhamilton road from Kinlough (R280), the great monolith of Eagles Rock appears to have been severed from the parent cliff by a Cyclopean sword. In reality, it is a good example of post-glacial slumping of the main cliff, after the supporting weight of the valley glacier had melted.

This route to Truskmore, the premier summit in Sligo, and on to the outlier of Tievebaun is via the inner sanctuary behind Eagles Rock. Leaving the R280 on the right at 797 512, use the single track road for 3.4km/2.1miles, which turns left over a bridge and continues towards the Rock. Park at or near the gate on your right, beside a tin-roofed hut.

Behind the hut and above a ruined cottage gable, rising ground takes you to the base of Eagles Rock. It is a stiff pull up the scree between its towering walls and the main cliff, where a jumble of boulders leads to a col. The rocks jutting crazily above resemble the ruins of some titanic castle, and frame views of Glenade Lough. Descend the stable blocks to the south, and traverse the grassy slope beneath a spur, towards two belts of conifers. Looking back, Eagles Rock displays three rock towers against the sky. Keep the height as you approach the lowest part of the escarpment, above a thin fringe of oak and birch trees. After negotiating a rock band, you angle up to the plateau rim.

Your ascent southwest is over heather, towards Truskmore (*Trusc Mor*, the Big Cod Fish: 644m/2,113ft) and its TV mast erected in the early 1960s. The mountain is capped with a layer of the Yoredale type sandstone, after you pick your way through boulders to the broad summit and the OS pillar beyond the mast. A panorama can be enjoyed over the nearby Gleniff Valley, the Benbulbin plateau and much of the Sligo coastline.

On the north side you descend through boulders to follow the ditch, marking the county boundary between Sligo and Leitrim, which further on becomes a wall. Where it turns sharp left, keep straight on and bear slightly right to the small cairn on Tievebaun (*Taobh Ban*, White Side: 612m/2,007ft). You have views west to Benwhiskin's cliffed edge across Gleniff. High up on the southwest side of the valley is the large opening of Diarmid and Grainne's cave. It is an outstanding feature and the key to a series of large caverns, formed from a long abandoned underground water course.

A few steps east of the summit, you overlook the lovely sweep of Glenade, with the Keeloges escarpment on the opposite side. The plateau edge is now followed south for a little, where you gradually angle towards a black patch of shale and stones on a lower terrace. Now zigzag down steep grass to meet the end of a green track. This leads out through a gate to a broader track to the approach road. The great fang of the Eagles Rock assumes changing shapes as you progress downhill. On joining the road, turn right to return to the starting point.

Distance: 9.6km/6miles. Ascent: 730m/2,400ft. Walking time: 4–4½ hours.

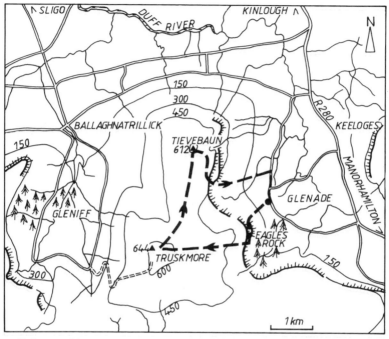

Reference OS Map: Sheet 16 (1:50,000).

44. THE DARTRY HILLS

This walk explores the lonely Dartry hills between Lough Melvin and Glenade in Co. Leitrim. The highlights again are the dramatic cliffs which abruptly terminate parts of their northern and north-western sides. Brooding over Leitrim's short coastline, they also form the conspicuous hinterland behind the resort of Bundoran in south Donegal. The underlying limestone is capped with later deposits of Yoredale sandstone and makes for surprisingly rolling moorland, with a central depression southwest of Lough Aroo.

From Kinlough (*Cionn an Locha*, Head of the Lake), south of Bundoran, take the Rossinver road (R281) along the south shore of Lough Melvin, turning right after 4.5km/2.8miles. Drive up an adequate road for 2km/ 1.3miles via some hairpin bends towards the summit of Glenaniff. Park beside the bridge (859 517) where a plantation ends on your left.

Use the bog track to the west towards the first shoulder which masks the unnamed top of 524m/1,720ft. From the first rise, keep to the edge of the cliffs to the high point just north and below the summit. Below you, a series of detached portions of the former edge have collapsed as gigantic landslips, a characteristic feature of these limestone plateaux.

There are commanding views over most of Lough Melvin and Donegal Bay. The summit cairn and attendant OS pillar extend the vista southwards over the rest of your route. Continuing in a southwest direction, gradually descend into a wide valley, and then ascend to Keeloges, (453m/1,487ft) with its vertical nose. The knob-like summit lies north of an oval lough with a white shingle beach — a place to freshen up on a hot day.

Now walk along the airy crest above the cliffs and gullies overlooking Glenade. On the opposite side, the Eagles Rock is backed by similar scarped edges of the Benbulbin range. Aprons of grey scree contrast with the bright green grass, below the gullies. At a point where you can view the whole of Glenade Lough, you can descend to previously left transport on the Kinlough-Manorhamilton road (R280) for a shorter day. Otherwise, the return walk is across the extensive tract of moorland, keeping the small scarped outcrops on your left. Further on, a slight drop takes you into a shallow basin with a sheep pen (the only fencing on this entire walk), where the terrain then continues to high ground around the shores of the crescentic Lough Aroo. A cairned top to the north is a southern spur of the 524m/1,720ft summit.

Northeast from the lough, your route descends to haggy ground around a small lochan. The final stages back to the starting point lead down a small valley to meet a bog track which is followed to a ford over a stream. Turn left and walk along the track to join the Glenaniff road at the bridge.

Distance: 12.8km/8miles. Ascent: 450m/1,500ft. Walking time: 5 hours.

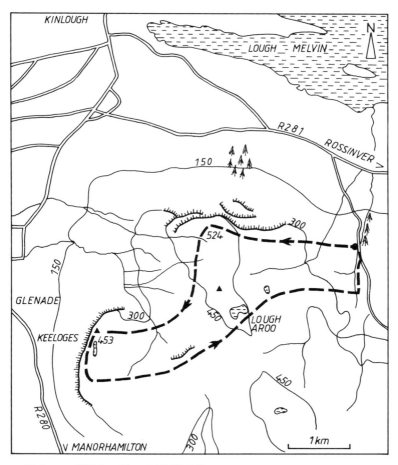

Reference OS Map: Sheet 16 (1:50,000).

45. BIG DOG FOREST

Sparsely populated west Fermanagh, with its four State forests of Navar, Conagher, Big Dog and Ballintempo, forms a veritable sea of conifers occupying the limestone uplands between Lower Lough Erne and Lough Macnean Upper. This walk follows a section of the Ulster Way, exploring the more interesting northern part of Big Dog Forest. Containing eight loughs, it is situated south of the unclassified road between Derrygonnelly and Garrison, on the shores of Lough Melvin.

Travel west from Derrygonnelly, using the Doagh route to Garrison (there is a more northerly route via Glennasheevar). Beyond Doagh Lough the road climbs between limestone hills, passing a small car park and the Ulster Way sign on your right. Continue along this road for a further 2km/1.5miles, which is the route of the Fermanagh Lakeland Way section of the Ulster Way. Park near a farm on the left, with a pair of swans on the gate pillars.

Walking downhill past the farm, you enter Big Dog Forest across a bridge and gate. The conspicuous top of Little Dog, with its viewing tower, overlooks the area. The track rises gently through the trees. Sitka spruce predominates, with other species such as pine and fir making up the balance. Keep straight on at a T–junction, passing Doo Lough (Black Lough) hidden by the trees on the left. Lough Nabrickboy (Lough of the Yellow Rising Ground) is split in two by the track. I had a rare daylight sighting of a badger, seeking refuge in a drain alongside the track at this spot.

Across the lough, use the narrow path which takes you to Little Dog viewpoint. An acropolis-like flight of steps leads to the 247m/810ft summit above Meenagleragh Lough. Its relative isolation, along with the neighbouring Big Dog, gives a wide panorama. Westwards, over Lough Melvin, the sharp edge of the Dartry Mountains rises south of Bundoran. Donegal Bay glints in the distance, its north shore guarded by Slieve League. Northwards, the conifers stretch away to Navar and the top of the Cliffs of Magho. The recumbent Cuilcagh, straddling the Fermanagh-Cavan border, fills the southeast scene.

Returning down the steps, follow the arrowed posts towards Big Dog. Waist-high heather on the northern side is best avoided by using a path, contouring up the east side to a limestone block at 259m/848ft. Both summits are supposedly named after Finn McCool's greyhounds, Sgeolan and Bran, who were bold enough to chase a doe, which was really a witch in disguise. In her anger, she changed the unfortunate hounds into a pair of hills.

Descend the same way, following the forest perimeter around to a marker post, where a path leads through the conifers past a ruined cottage. It rises to a wider track, to join the road between Derrygonnelly and Cashel Cross Roads. Walking east from here, you pass a gated forest road on your left, where the Ulster Way meanders south. Further on, turn left immediately past Rossinure House into Big Dog Forest car part and picnic site.

Your return route now proceeds north, along the forest track to Lough Nabrickboy. It is worth diverting on to a path at the arrowed post along the shore to Doo Lough in its miniature highland setting, backed by the heathery ridge of Trustia (288m/944ft). Follow the path for a short distance along the picturesque shore, where it ascends left to rejoin the track leading back to the forest entrance.

Distance: 8km/5miles. Ascent: 120m/400ft. Walking time: 2¼ hours.

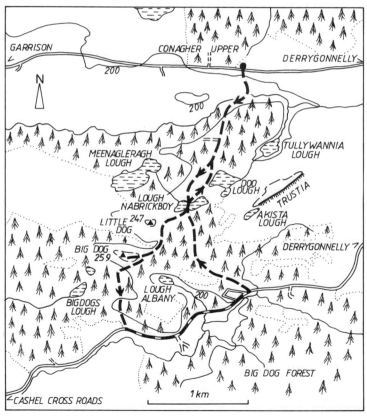

Reference OSNI Map: Sheet 17 (1:50,000).

46. THE LOUGH DERG HILLS: CROCKKINNAGOE-GROUSEHALL HILL

Lough Derg (Red Lake) is Donegal's largest; it has a 21km/13miles circumference and occupies a schist basin. It is tucked away in the remote and sparsely populated southeast corner of the county, close to the Northern Ireland border. The lough has an association with St Patrick that goes back to the fifth century, and thousands of pilgrims are attracted annually to Station Island between 1 June and 15 August.

The walk to the two summits described here, lying to the east of the lough, is only rarely made. Crockkinnagoe gives a grandstand view of the penitential boat traffic plying between Station Island and the shore during the summer months.

Take the Lough Derg road (R233) from Pettigoe as far as the Y-junction marked Lough Derg, 3km. Bear right and continue for 2km/1.5miles up the east side of the lough to a point opposite Station Island at 101 703.

Crockkinnagoe's summit (364m/1,194ft) rises to the southeast. Except in the driest summer weather, the initial stages will be a bit squelchy over the tussock grass and bog to the end of the conifers at the base of Meenna-gassagh Hill. Follow the right-hand bank of the stream flowing out of the tiny Lough Nashannagh. Further on, cross the fence on the left-hand side, where firm ground leading to the summit opens up a vista of Lough Nashannagh, backed by the west end of Lower Lough Erne and the limestone plateaus of Leitrim and Sligo. The OS cairn has the date 1948 on its plinth. From here, we can survey an expansive view of Lough Derg with some twenty-five islands and islets. The great Basilica, consecrated in 1931, with its turquoise dome and attendant buildings, completely covers Station Island and floats serenely on the waters of the lough. The once bare scene to the northwest is now covered with a vast carpet of conifers, stretching away towards the Barnesmore Hills with the Blue Stack range to the left. Further west, high ground can be followed all the way to Slieve League. Southwards, the Cuilcagh ridge forms the back-drop to the whole Lough Erne basin, with Boa Island, the largest island inside Ireland.

This most isolated 300m/1,000ft summit in the county is unique, in that one looks north over a western extension of Co. Tyrone and back again into Donegal. The River Derg, flowing out of the lough's northeast corner is concealed by plantations. In the far north you can identify all the hills from Inishowen right round to Slieve Snaght (Derryveagh).

Your route now descends, at first north, and then northeast towards the modest Grousehall Hill (approx. 300m/1,000ft) almost surrounded by conifers. The ground levels out where you cross the forest access road and continue past Acheson's Lough. Young trees have been planted right to the summit, which will in time block out the similar panorama as seen from Crockkinnagoe.

A short drain-hopping descent now leads down through a narrow belt of trees, where the main plantation boundary fence is followed southwest for a short distance to reach the access road. Follow it downhill and through a pair of wooden gates. Turn right, and follow the stream to lower ground, over two fences (the lower one has a stile). Bear slightly left to join up with the outward route leading back to the starting point.

Distance: 8.8km/5.5miles. Ascent: 210m/700ft. Walking time: 3 hours.

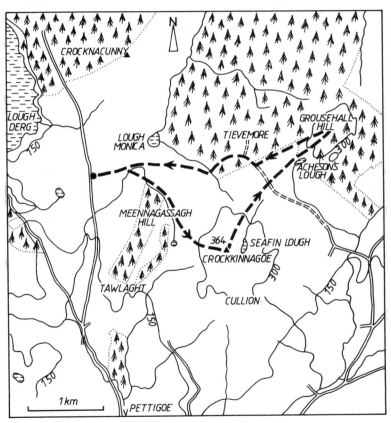

Reference OSNI Map: Sheet 12 (1:50,000).

This is a wild and rugged area of granite uplands north of Lough Eske (Loch Eisc, Lake of Fish). Forming the largest knot of high ground in Donegal, there are few traces of man on these hills — no fences, walls or walkers' paths. Five summits exceed 610m/2,000ft, only two of which are named on the OS map. In the vicinity of Lough Eske along the main road to Donegal Town, their subdued summits are difficult to distinguish. What they lack in stature and individuality however, is made up for in the display of interesting glacially eroded landforms. Wherever approached, the Blue Stacks will subject the walker to rough, tough and sometimes very boggy conditions.

The described walk explores the area around Lough Belshade (*Loch béal séad*, River mouth with the Jewels). It commences at the end of a single track road, north of Edergole Bridge. The approach road leaves the N15 southwest of Barnesmore Gap and continues to the head of Lough Eske via its eastern side. Turn right at the top of the hairpin bend and park after 1km/0.6miles beside a barn (970 871) with a walkers' indicator post nearby.

The rough track passes a plantation, falls to cross a stream and continues uphill. Since 1989, the former rather marshy track has been improved and extended up to the river behind the Eas Doonan waterfall, during the construction phase of a small private hydro scheme. This diverts water from the Corabber River (but not enough to dry up the waterfall, even after prolonged dry spells) via a buried pipeline to a power house concealed in the plantation at the head of Lough Eske. From the sluice gate at the top of the track it is worth diverting to the right to view the cascade, which plunges into a black pool at the end of a small gorge containing rare ferns.

Above the falls, follow the left bank of the Corabber, meandering in its grassy valley, passing a few marker posts. You then ascend a rough path up the left bank of a stream draining Lough Belshade. The new small stone weir across the outlet of the lough has raised the surface a little. The buttresses of granite rising above the north shore were once the nesting sites of some of Ireland's last golden eagles. Legend has it that a black cat guards a crock of gold within the boundaries of this tarn.

Your route along the south shore passes a heather-clad island to the base of a stream descending from the ridge to the left of the buttresses. Follow it up into the wild ice-scratched basin, which displays an impressive area of grooved rock and provides a welcome diversion for the scrambler. Bearing slightly right, above the buttresses, this superbly rocky ascent leads to the cairn on Ardnageer (*Ard-na-geer*, Height of the Berries: 642m/2,118ft). After admiring the panorama over the neighbouring summits, a descent to the east takes you over an expanse of bare granite littered with rocks, and past a large precariously perched boulder overlooking a rock tarn. Beyond this, the ground drops into a trench and then ascends the rock-strewn hillside to the summit of Croaghbann (*Cruach beann*, Rounded Hill: 641m/2,000ft).

The descent to the south is over a mixture of rocks and heather, passing the head of the Owendoo Valley which is flanked by the Croaghbarnes ridge. With Loughinisland and Lough Fad on the left, continue the descent to the southeast corner of Lough Belshade and retrace your steps down the outlet stream to the Corabber Valley and hence back to Edergole.

Distance: 12 km/7.5miles. Ascent: 640m/2,100ft. Walking time: 4½ hours.

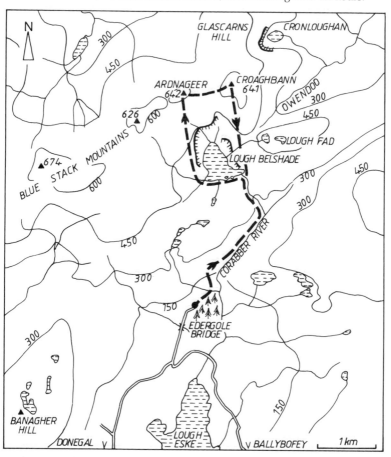

Reference OS Map: Sheet 11 (1:50,000).

48. THE BLUE STACK FIVE

This round of the five Blue Stack summits exceeding 610m/2,000ft includes Glascarns Hill (Glascharn, Green Carn or Monument: 533m/ 1,750ft) as a starter. The walk commences from the disused school (960 940) in the Reelan valley on the north side of the range.

Using the R253 road from Ballybofey to Glenties, drive west from Reelan Bridge for 5km/3.3miles, passing the quartzite cone of Gaugin. Above the plantations, turn left at 966 963 onto a single track road. Continue for 3.5km/2.2miles to the old school on the right, just beyond a left turn (downhill) to Crolack farm, in its oasis of trees across the river.

The rumpled arc of the Blue Stacks is all around you, and a rewarding day lies ahead. The ascent to Glascarns Hill starts from the bridge leading to Crolack, and is a straightforward toil over two rises. Protruding granite nearer the top makes the going easier, until you arrive at the cairn on a rock outcrop. You can survey the Owengarve valley to the east, with Altnapaste hill in the background.

With much of the ascent behind you (until you get to Sruell Gap), proceed south, above Cronloughan corrie, to Croaghbann (610m/2,000ft), with its summit lakelet, Lough Aduff. The section from here to Ardnageer, which takes you past the large perched boulder is a reverse of the previous walk from Lough Belshade.

From Ardnageer, there is a featureless stretch of ground, leading past the conspicuous white quartz outcrop and on over rough terrain to the Blue Stack summit. If there is the slightest hint of mist on this section, the map and compass should be conveniently to hand. If clear conditions prevail, however, you can divert from the higher ground on your left, and look for the scant remains of a Sunderland aircraft which crashed in January 1944. Its location is about 0.5km/0.25miles northeast of the south cairn on Blue Stack, below the ridge and overlooking Croaghanard Lough. Parts of the wreckage, which lay around a stream, were removed in 1990 to a local history museum in Glenties.

Regaining the ridge, the south cairn reveals the whole of Lough Eske and the drumlin country around Donegal Bay. The official summit to the north, at 676m/2,219ft, gives a magnificent panorama which embraces much of Donegal. Slieve League and Slievetooey dominate the west, while northwards, over the intervening ridges, are the familiar outlines of Slieve Snaght, Errigal and Muckish.

A gradual descent to the northwest takes you to Sruell Gap (*Bearna na Struthal*, Gap of Swift Streams: 480m/1,600ft approx.). This was the route used by bare-footed pilgrims, travelling up the Sruell valley on their way to Doon Well (*Tobar a' Duin*) near Churchill. On the right-hand side of the valley is the fine waterfall of the Grey Mare's Tail. It translates in Irish however, as the White Mare's Tail (*Scardan na Larna Baine*). A stiff pull takes you up the green slopes of Lavagh More (*Leamhach*, Place of Elms:

674m/2,211ft), where the cairn gives views to the main ridge. Both Lavagh More and Lavagh Beg are composed of softer schist rocks. A slight descent northwest is followed by the final grassy shoulder to Lavagh Beg (610m/2,000ft) which cradles a pair of tiny lakelets. Your outlook is high over the upper reaches of the Reelan valley.

The descent to the northeast is at first over steep grass, leading through lower peaty ground towards a yellow-roofed barn near the river. Here, you join a track leading over a bridge to meet the rough road to Glenties. Walk down the road for 2.4km/1.5miles to the old school.

Distance: 16km/10miles. Ascent: 760m/2,500ft. Walking time: 6–7 hours.

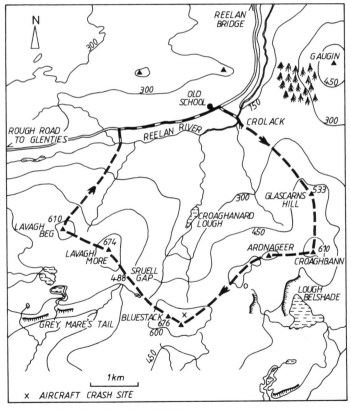

Reference OS Map: Sheet 11 (1:50,000).

49. SLIEVE LEAGUE

Slieve League (Sliabh liag, Mountain of the Flagstones: 601m/1,972ft) broods over the south Donegal coast. On your approach road (R263) west of Killybegs, it appears as a relatively unassuming lump, giving no indication of its dramatic ocean frontage. There are a number of approaches to the summit, including that via Lough Agh on the northern side, or by the Pilgrim Track past Croleavy Lough to the holy well below the east summit, which is signposted (Sliabh Liag) *off the Teelin road.*

The classic and most popular route which traverses the whole exhilarating crest of the mountain, and the one which draws most walkers time and time again, begins from the car park, perched on the 240m/800ft headland of Bunglass (*Bunglas,* End of the Green). The access road starts from Teelin, 3km/2miles south of Carrick. Ignore the sign mentioned earlier, just before the village, as this points the way to the less scenic Pilgrim Track. Turning right at Teelin for Bunglass (3km/2miles), an adventurous road ascends towards the jagged skyline, giving a foretaste of what lies ahead. In its final stages you traverse the steep hillside high above the sea, with the old signal tower on Carrigan Head on the left. Over the last rise, the road terminates beyond Lough O'Mulligan at the car park.

A few steps around the corner at a spot known as *Amharc Mor* (Great View) reveal Slieve League's gigantic facade. Its huge face, extending for some 3km/2miles has been fashioned by the remorseless Atlantic, whittling away at the base of the cliffs over aeons of time. The multi-coloured hues of the schists, slates, quartzites and conglomerates, combined with various mineral ores and the natural vegetation, produce a kaleidoscope of colours. Slieve League is the *pièce de résistance* of the Irish coast. Its only possible rival is the slightly higher Croaghaun cliffs on Achill Island. But they lack the variety of form, and are nowhere displayed to perfection, having no natural balcony like Bunglass.

The actual summit lies west of the dipped arête, which some maps refer to as the 'One Man's Pass'. The rather colourful description in an early guidebook of 'a narrow footway high in the air, with awful abysses yawning on either side' will not daunt today's seasoned walker. A short rib of rock (as illustrated in volume 2 of *Climbing in the British Isles* by H.C. Hart) north of Crockrawer can claim to be the truer 'One Man's Pass'.

Leaving Bunglass, ascend the path, meandering up through crags and heather to Scregeighter (*Screagioctar,* Lower Rocky Ground: 311m/1,021ft). It then follows the elbow of the cliffs over the vertical section of the Eagle's Nest (450m/1,500ft), which *requires caution* in high winds. Far below, white horses surge and suck at the foot of the Giant's Desk and Chair — a pair of sea stacks. The path then drops a little, before rising to contour the slopes of Crockrawer (*Cnocreamhar,* Fat Hill).

Continuing up the cliffed edge, the rib of the 'One Man's Pass' is seen above some projections. Angling up for around 10m/30ft with a

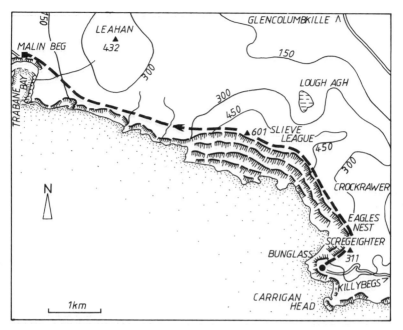

Reference OS Map: Sheet 10 (1:50,000).

precipitous drop on the seaward side, it will not perturb anyone used to heights, and it can be bypassed on the landward side. Further up, along the crest, past a vertical bluff, grand views extend eastwards over Teelin Harbour to St John's Point. Diverging a little to the north from here takes you to the site of the oratory and wells associated with Saint Assicus, who was a goldsmith to Saint Patrick. This lofty place of worship had its last special pilgrimage in 1909.

Regaining height again, walk over the boulder field, passing the cairn on the east summit. Beyond this, the ground falls slightly to cross the arête above the corrie containing Lough Agh. The gullies above the lough are reputed to support a colony of Alpine plants. The level walk across this One Man's Pass presents few difficulties, after which a short rise leads to the OS pillar, which is an unsurpassed belvedere in clear weather.

Your view is high over Donegal Bay, which is backed by the limestone uplands in Fermanagh and Sligo, and right along to Benwee Head and the Stags of Broadhaven in outermost Mayo. Inland lies the hump of Nephin, and exceptional visibility will reveal conical Croagh Patrick, 120km/75miles away. Northwards, over the back of the Slievetooey and Glengesh heights, the unmistakable screes of Errigal and the dome of Slieve Snaght top the northern horizon. Westwards, Rathlin O'Birne Island forms a cornerstone to this delectable coast. A short distance from the summit, where the ridge drops to the west, a series of residual sandstone pinnacles known as the Chimneys invite exploration. They are about 60m/200ft below, on the very steep seaward side. Monuments to a vast denudation, they make statuesque foregrounds for the adventurous photographer.

The natural extension to this walk (if not returning to Bunglass) is to descend the west side, following the coast for about 4km/2.5miles to Trabane Bay (*Traig ban*, White Strand), known as the Silver Strand. You can also make a detour to take in Leahan (432m/1,418ft). Return transport would have to be previously left at the car park (497 800) at the top of the long flight of steps that leads up from the beach.

Distance (summit walk): 9.6km/6miles. Ascent: 360m/1,200ft. Walking time: 3½ hours.

Distance (Bunglass-Trabane Bay): 14.4km/9miles. Ascent: 570m/1,900ft. Walking time: 5 hours.

50. GLEN HEAD — STURRALL

Glencolumbkille (Gleann Cholm Cille, St Columba's Valley) has long associations with the Saint, and is situated at the seaward end of the most westerly valley in Donegal. The area possesses a wealth of historical antiquities and one of the few fertile strips on this inhospitable coast. With the village as a base, the locality is something of a Mecca for the aspiring archaeologist and the explorer of superb cliff scenery. Inexpensive accommodation is available at Dooey Hostel and the Malinmore Adventure Centre.

The view of Glen Head, the bold headland terminating the north side of the valley, is foreshortened on the approach road from Killybegs and Carrick (R263). Further along the road towards Malinmore however, its 244m/800ft ochre-coloured face towers over Glen Bay, backed by the residual wedge of the Sturrall (*Sturric*, Pinnacle).

This compact walk gives an introduction to all of this wild coast. Turn left at the T–junction at the north end of the village and proceed for 2.5km/1.6miles, passing the Church of Ireland and its ancient cross-pillar (one of fifteen stations associated with Columba). Keeping straight on at the next junction, the road crosses the Garveross River (*Garbh-ros*, Rough Point [of land]), and continues around the valley. Park near a cottage under the craggy slopes of Beefan and Garveross Mountain (279m/916ft). Sir Arnold Bax, the composer, during thirty years association with Glencolumbkille, where many of his works were written, described Beefan as 'a glittering many-coloured surface of rock, bracken and heather'.

A rough track winds up Glen Head gaining height rapidly above the contorted cliffs around Skelpoonagh Bay. There are views over the valley to the thatched roofs of the Folk Village, which are reminiscent of how all the cottages would have once looked. Leaving the track which continues north, bear left and walk across heathery ground to the old signal tower. This is one of the better preserved of a chain of twelve, built in great haste in the early 1800s to guard the coast against a supposed invasion by Napoleon.

You have an oceanic outlook high over Glen Bay to Rossan Point, backed by Rathlin O'Birne Island. Northwards, beyond the deserted harbour at Port, the view is restricted by the bulk of Slievetooey and Croaghballaghdown. Now follow the sheer cliff high above the inaccessible cove of Camas Binne (bent cliff). In October, 1870, the cargo ship 'Sydney' foundered here with a load of timber en route from Quebec to Greenock. Twenty-seven of the crew perished with only a few managing to struggle up these cliffs to safety. Descending to the right into a small valley, walk over short turf to regain the cliff edge, until you reach the narrow neck connecting the Sturrall with the mainland. Its stupendous face looks impossibly steep, even for grazing sheep, though surprisingly I spotted one during a visit for this guide. As there is no apparent way across the exposed and shattered crest, the 'back door' to the main top (a blunt

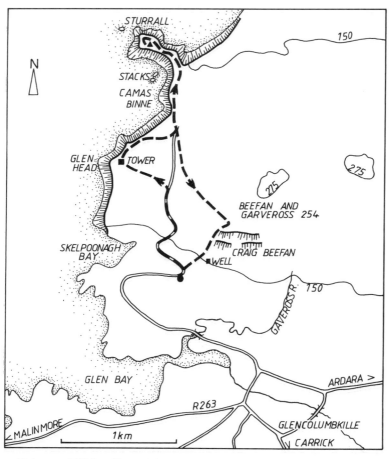

Reference OS Map: Sheet 10 (1:50,000).

pinnacle) is by an adrenalin-producing traverse along the less awesome north side. I would hesitate in recommending it to anyone without a good head for heights.

Keeping the same level as the neck, *excercise care on this section*. The ground is not unduly difficult as you pass below the quartzite wall on your left, after which you angle up to climb over a stone sheep barrier. A scramble up to the left takes you to a small hollow with some fallen blocks. Turning the corner to the right, there is a slight descent, followed by a heather slope on the left, leading to the highest point.

Your dizzy perch has no peer on this coast. With an abysmal drop of 180m/600ft on the south side, the majestic Glen Head and the distant Slieve League hold the scene across Camas Binne. On an elemental day the waves exploding relentlessly at the base of the cliffs echo the words of the poet Shelley:

> Around
> Whose caverned base the whirlpools and the waves
> Bursting and eddying irresistibly
> Rage and resound for ever.

It is not possible to proceed along the knife-edge without a rope, so return carefully by the outward route. From the main cliffs, follow a sheep track to the head of the small valley, until a bog track is met. Turn left (uphill) for a short distance and then bear right and ascend to the flat summit of Beefan and Garveross. From above the south side which is all short cliffs, gullies and scree, you can view all of the Glencolumbkille Valley.

Take a south-westerly descent, avoiding the crags and look for a bank of stones below you, between the bracken-covered knolls. This is a long rectangular cairn, with St Columba's Well set in a recess and topped by a cross-pillar. A nearby plaque indicates it is the Turas Cholmcille, Stad 7 (Columcille's Journey, Station 7). From the well it is a short descent to your starting point.

Distance: 7.2km/4.5miles. Ascent: 240m/800ft. Walking time: 2½ hours.

51. SLIEVETOOEY

Between Maghera (Machaire, plain) and Glencolumbkille, some 24km/15miles of the iron-bound coast thrusting into the Atlantic was considered *by the late Joey Glover of the North West Mountaineering Club to be 'a gourmet's route and a lengthy day, taking in some of Donegal's magnificent cliff scenery'. This particular route along a heritage quality coastline, offers a superb combination of jagged rocks, stacks, cliffs, bays and promontories. Murray's 1912* Guide to Ireland *stated that all this coast between Teelin and Maghera could 'hardly be excelled by any locality in the British Isles'. Thankfully it still remains remote, inviolate and challenging today.*

The equally exhilarating walk described here, starts from Maghera, ascends Croaghballaghdown (Hill Pass of the Fort: 516m/1,692ft) and continues over Slievetooey (*Sliabh tuaith*, Northern Mountain: 462m/1,515ft) to return via the cliffs.

You reach Maghera by turning right, off the N56, south of Ardara (Maghera Caves 8km/5.25miles). The scenic road passes the Assarnacally waterfall and on to Maghera's scattered houses at the foot of the sinister Owenwee or Granny's Glen, once notorious for poteen-makers. Park beyond the last cottage in a small disused quarry on the right (659 903).

Climb steeply to the ruins of the ancient promontory fort, 'Maghera Castle', which faces up the tidal sweep of Loughros Beg Bay. You now follow a fence, bearing left to ascend through quartzite crags to the first top of Croaghacruppan, with views to the head of Owenwee Glen. The gradient eases as you ascend to the broad ridge which is followed up to the OS pillar on Croaghballagh down, the walk's high point.

On a classic summer's day, the eye ranges over the deep sapphire blue of Lough Croaghballaghdown in the corrie below you, and out over the Loughros and Dawros peninsulas. Arranmore Island and the Bloody Foreland lie beyond the azure expanse of Gweebarra Bay.

Follow the ridge west down to a col, then climb to a small cairn at the eastern end of the Slievetooey plateau. It is higher than pt 444m/1,458ft to the west, beyond which you continue across eroded peat, passing Lough Awoty. A short climb then takes you to the main cairn.

Here, you look over the lonely Glenlough valley, with its river spilling on to a stony and barely accessible beach. Offshore, the huge bastion of Tormore and its entourage of lesser stacks are overlooked by Port Hill. In the background, the Sturrall's eroded crest is connected to the mainland just north of Glen Head, capped by the old signal tower.

Your descent to the north, at first over stony ground, terminates at the cliff edge, which plunges 300m/1,000ft at this point. *Excercise care* as you move eastwards along the rim. On a stormy day this is Atlantic Ireland at its wildest. The stupendous cliffs excel Slieve League for verticality and in places the crumbling edge testifies to the ongoing erosion, where vast slabs of quartzite have peeled away. The shingle beaches far below are used as hauling out refuges for seals.

Offshore stacks and skerries accompany you as far as the broad green Gull Island. Despite its name, there is a general paucity of sea birds frequenting this coast. Now drop to cross a little ravine cut by the stream issuing from Lough Adoocho, after which there is the option of keeping strictly to the lesser cliffs or taking the more direct line across the open slopes. The latter route crosses the stream draining Lough Croaghballagh-down. Further on, a narrow sheep path threads through some hillocks to a col, where Maghera beach comes into view. Descend and contour the hillside towards the beach. Interesting plants such as goldenrod, roseroot and purple saxifrage flourish in this area.

Look carefully for the tenuous sheep path traversing the hillside beyond a bracken-filled hollow. It is a little exposed in places and *requires caution*. Immediately past a small stream in a mossy crevice, the path angles up to the right, over a rock band, to take a higher route. The base of the cliffed hillside under you is perforated by half-a-dozen caves, accessible at low spring tide. The most interesting is *Cooach a' Darchadass*, or Dark Cave, reputed to be the longest. Continue along the path to a fence at the cliff edge above the beach. Here you descend to the sand dunes, bearing right for Maghera at the end of a rewarding day.

Distance: 17.6km/11miles. Ascent: 640m/2,100ft. Walking time: 6 hours.

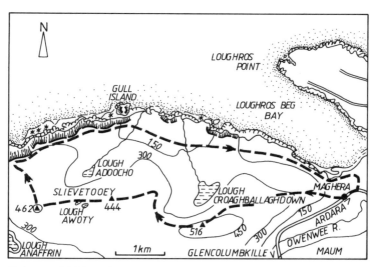

Reference OS Map: Sheet 10 (1:50,000).

52. THE GLENGESH HILLS

Glengesh (Gleann geis, Glen of the Swans) is one of two glaciated valleys that sculpture the northern edge of the Banagh peninsula. The steeply plunging flank of Common Mountain on the glen's south side shows to advantage on the N56 approach road from Glenties. The glen carries the road between Ardara and Carrick to a height of 270m/900ft over Glengesh Pass via a couple of hairpin bends.

This walk traverses the three summits above the glen, commencing from the school layby on the Carrick road. Access is by turning right off the N56, south of Ardara at Common Bridge, and a short distance up the glen parking space is available at the school on the right.

Walk up the road for approximately 0.8km/0.5miles, where a track on the right leads to the second thatched cottage on the slopes of Glengesh Hill. Cross the fence to the left and ascend the hillside, which reveals the length of the glen, threaded by the Glengesh River. Continue your ascent by a stream above a fenced-off track. Southwards, the craggy spur of Common Mountain broods over the Neck of the Ballagh. Glengesh Hill's undistinguished summit (393m/1,291ft) lies back from the rim of the glen across broken ground, commanding a panoramic view northwards over the Loughros and Dawros peninsulas and right up the west coast.

Now walk over the haggy ground, back towards the glen. There are glimpses down to Maghery beach, backed by the heights of Slievetooey. Stay above the several rock outcrops and thus avoid the damper lower ground. Further on, you descend to a stream crossed by an old track, and the terrain then ascends the eastern slope of Croaghavehy (*Croagh a' behy*, Hill of the Birch: 74m/1,228ft). A modern conifer plantation which you pass on the left has replaced any birches which may have graced this hill in the past. From the cairnless summit the noble sweep of Glengesh frames a distant view of the Glendowan and Fintown hills.

An easy descent takes you towards the top of the Pass, where you cross the road between the hairpin bends and another small plantation. Drop into the little ravine cut by the infant Glengesh River, and then a mostly grassy ascent of around 200m/700ft leads to Common Mountain. Approaching the summit, you will notice that extensive areas of grass cover have been stripped away by natural erosion, possibly aggravated by overgrazing. The third highest trig. point on Banagh gives a spatial vista over southwest Donegal which is dominated by Slieve League. To the northeast, you look over a bowl-shaped valley to Ardara, with the massed heights of the Blue Stacks filling the eastern skyline.

Departing from your last summit, descend the northern spur of Common Mountain towards the precipitous rim of the glen and continue down the edge to the last farm on the south side of the Glengesh River. Cross the bridge leading to the farm to join the road, which in a short distance takes you back to the school.

Distance: 12.8km/8miles. Ascent: 762m/2,500ft. Walking time: 5 hours.

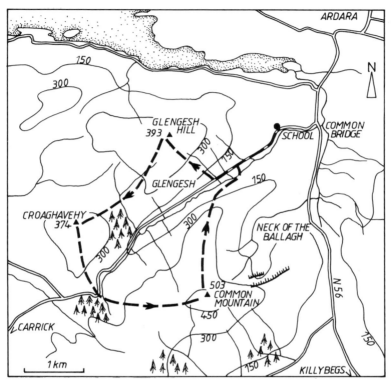

Reference OS Map: Sheet 10 (1:50,000).

53. AGHLA MOUNTAIN-KNOCKRAWER

Lough Finn in its glaciated trough is hemmed in on the south side by a range of hills extending towards Glenties. On the R252 approach road from Ballybofey, the highest of the group, Aghla Mountain (598m/1,961ft) is the whale-backed ridge to the left of its more conspicuous neighbour, Scraigs (430m/1,410ft).

You can start the ascent from the disused gravel quarry, excavated out of the glacial moraines at the southwest end of the lough, just off the road (now the R250) at 890 005. Pass the first farm at the end of the lough and continue towards the conifer plantation beyond a second farm on the alluvial fan at the base of the obvious gully. Leave the track before the farm at a marker post and climb up the left-hand side of the gully.

The ground rises steeply at first, through shaggy heather, then leading to more open terrain and revealing the entire length of Lough Finn. This takes its name from the legendary girl Finna, who was supposedly drowned in its dark waters while attempting to save her brother Fergoman, a local chieftain, from being attacked by an irate pig. Higher up, the gully divides into two. Continue above the waterfall in the left-hand one to reach the crest, where the first of a series of eroded quartzite tops lies to the left of two of the mountain's ten lochans.

Southwards, the prominent OS pillar indicates the main summit and the easiest route keeps the higher ground on the left. It gives good views south over Lough Ea (the source of the Owenea) to the rugged line of the Blue Stacks and their western outliers, while the dome of Slieve Snaght and the Glendowan hills will hold your gaze to the north. Westwards, beyond Glenties, the Dawros peninsula forms the south side of Gweebarra Bay.

Leaving the summit a gradual descent north-westwards over the undulating ridge leads to a stone cairn. Keeping Castle Lough and Lough Analtmore on your left, continue west to the unnamed lochan with a 450m/1,500ft top immediately to its west. This can be included before a drop and then a rise to Knockrawer (*Cnoc reamhar*, Fat or Thick Hill: 451m/1,481ft). Your final summit overlooks the broad Shallogans valley with its river. Faint traces of the Stranorlar-Glenties narrow gauge railway which closed in 1952 can be seen, alongside the R250.

The descent to the northeast crosses the Shruhanacrow More River, where the ground then rises over broken bog, below the screes on Sculloge. It soon levels out, and having crossed two fences, your route descends to the old gravel quarry at the end of Lough Finn.

Distance: 8km/5miles. Ascent: 490m/1,600ft. Walking time: 3–3½ hours.

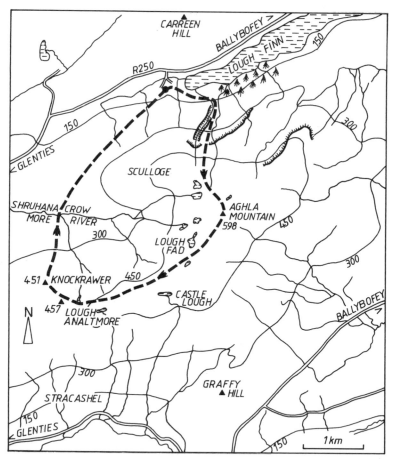

Reference OS Map: Sheet 11 (1:50,000).

54. SLIEVE SNAGHT (DERRYVEAGH)

On the approach road (R251) below Errigal, the granite dome of Slieve Snaght (Sliabh-sneachta, Mountain of the Snows: 683m/2,240ft) broods over the moorland south of Dunlewy and its luxuriant woods. It is flanked to its left by the sombre amphitheatre of the Poisoned Glen, whose glacially smoothed buttresses seamed with gullies invite exploration. There are a number of routes to the summit. The shorter ones, all commencing in the vicinity of Lough Barra on the south side, are more suitable for winter days.

The more classic approach described, and the more convenient for visitors staying at Dunlewy Hostel, takes the walker via the grand introduction of the Poisoned Glen. It then progresses into the hub of the Derryveaghs (*Doire bheathach*, Birch Wood) to savour an optimum combination of wild scenery, rushing rivers, crags and corrie lakes.

Commencing from the road bend (930 189) below the roofless Dunlewy church, use the short length of track which peters out beyond the old bridge over the Owenwee Burn. Continue up the glen between the enclosing hills, keeping to the left bank of the Cronaniv Burn. The glen may have derived its name from the poisonous Irish spurge (genus *Euphorbia*) reputed to have grown along the banks of the burn. Passing a solitary holly tree, keep the river on your right and cross it where it turns sharp left. Now ascend to the obvious low notch or 'window' on the granite crest, following up through heather and rock beside a small stream to enter a shallow gully. The fortress-like walls to either side were once the haunt of the eagle, but alas they have not been graced by the 'king of the birds' since the turn of the century. Emerging on to the ridge, bear right and ascend over rock and heather to pass Lough Maumbeg, a small tarn nestling in a rocky trench. Further up there is an unnamed cairned summit beyond which lies a larger tarn similar to Maumbeg. A further ascent leads to the summit known as Rocky Cap, with a steep gully to the north and an adjacent tarn.

The descent to the west down a rocky slope emerges on to the boulder-strewn platform north of Lough Slievesnaght followed by the final 180m/600ft ascent to the cairn on Slieve Snaght's broad summit. As the highest point in the main part of Glenveagh National Park (a separate portion includes part of Errigal) it is a superlative viewpoint. While the stately line of peaks from Errigal to Muckish will hold your gaze to the north, all the coastal features and islands from the Bloody Foreland to Tormore rock at the end of Slievetooey in the far southwest can be picked out.

Descend the steep northwest side, with its smooth slabs, to join the Devlin River at a point below the cascade on its exit from Lough Aganniv. Red deer (*Cervus elephas*) can be seen in this area. The ground levels out and by following the river closely on its right bank the worst of the peat hags can be avoided. The river divides around some islands about a mile further down before entering a shallow gorge which deepens as it descends towards Dunlewy. Rocky bluffs will prevent you keeping to the water's edge all the way through. The gorge in its sequestered highland setting is attractively fringed with oak and some rhododendron, and its refreshing pools will come as a welcome relief after a warm summer descent.

Further down, the river bears left to enter the Dunlewy woods, but you can keep straight on to cross the Cronaniv Burn. If this is in flood, it may be a case of boots off or else using the bridge a little downstream, leading to Dunlewy House.

Distance: 12.8km/8miles. Ascent: 730m/2,400ft. Walking time: 5 hours.

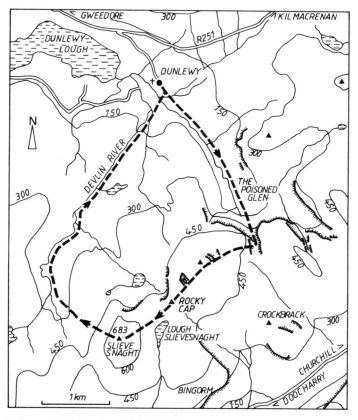

Reference OS Map: Sheet 1 (1:50,000).

55. ERRIGAL

The startling peak of Errigal (Aireagal, Oratory: 752m/2,466ft) dominates the Rosses country. The aspiring hill walker travelling from the south will have seen glimpses of its upper half, topping the intervening hills. In the vicinity of Gweedore, its pyramidal form, bedecked with frost-shattered scree, is always impressive. These dove-grey quartzite screes often give the illusion of snow, due to refracted light in bright sunshine. Part of the mountain's south side has been incorporated into the Glenveagh National Park.

There are two contrasting ascents to the twin summits. The popular 'tourist route' uses the easier southeast ridge, starting off the R251 where it climbs over moorland east of Dunlewy. The other more adventurous ascent is by the airy northwest ridge starting near a small farm (910 211) whose access road turns right (uphill) at McGeady's pub near Errigal youth hostel and continues for 2km/1.5miles. A winter's day on this ridge can be a real challenge as the world shrinks beneath you and the wind roars and buffets around the crags and you add another day to your experience.

To give a slightly longer day, the route described includes the northeastern satellite of Mackoght (490m/1,600ft) as an appetiser. Some travel writers have erroneously referred to it as 'Little Errigal'. Park at the ruined gateway on the R251 at Carlaghmohane Bridge (952 205) where a faint track leads to the derelict Altan Farm.

Walk up the track, leaving it where it swings right, and then ascend Mackoght's lower slopes. Steep ground continues above a line of old fencing posts and then over quartzite outcrops to the summit cairn perched above the precipitous west face. You have a magnificent prospect of Errigal, which eclipses all its neighbours for dramatic sharpness of form. The entire northeast face, smothered in a chaos of loose scree, displays erosional disintegration on the grand scale. The 'tourist route' can be traced up the skyline ridge.

Leaving the summit, descend through rocks and heather to the broad col between Mackoght and Errigal. A series of moraines below the north side look as fresh as when the last ice-sheets melted. The uncompromising climb leads unerringly up the well-scratched track, unfolding a widening panorama. The scalloped face of Aghla Mor or Little Errigal, rising from Altan Lough, heads an entourage of peaks northwards to Muckish. Higher up, past a jutting rock fang, the track turns around the end of the summit ridge to emerge at a circular enclosure to the left of the Glover memorial cairn (erected 1978).

The ridge now dwindles to a narrow crest, providing a degree of exposure, especially under snow. It terminates at the eastern and higher of the twin summits, which is arguably the smallest in Ireland. A short 'one man's path' connects it with the western twin. The highest point in the northwest has a great feeling of aloofness, and on a good day is a breathtaking vantage point. The all-embracing view covers Donegal, its fretted coast and islands and more than half of Ulster. At one's feet lie the shimmering loughs of Dunlewy and Nacung, divided by a causeway. The stern granite surrounding the plummeting gullies of the Poisoned Glen together with the dome of Slieve Snaght resemble 'the wrinkled hide of a petrified elephant' and form a savage backdrop to the whole Dunlewy scene.

It is best to return by the 'tourist route'. You do not need to follow the line of unnecessary marker posts leading to the road from below Mackoght col. A more direct line can be taken further east to join the road a little to the west of the starting point.

Distance: 7.2km/4.5miles. Ascent: 650m/2,131ft. Walking time: 3½ hours.

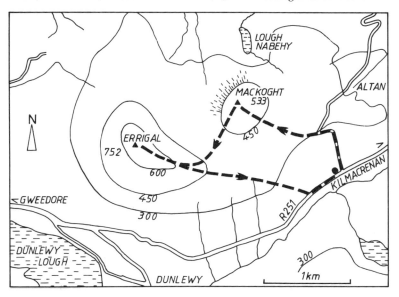

Reference OS Map: Sheet 1 (1:50,000).

56. THE AGHLAS

The elegant cone of Aghla More (Eachla, Stable) or Little Errigal broods over the north shore of the secretive Altan Lough (Altan, Little Cliff). With Aghla Beg's twin tops, the trio forms the middle section of the grand promenade known as the 'Glover Highlander'. This rewarding day's walk from Muckish to Errigal has become an annual event, held in September.

The approach to these hills can be made either from the south, via the scant track leading to Altan Farm off the R251 at 952 205, or via the forest track off the Muckish Gap road (003 257). A clockwise route involving none of these longer approaches commences at the fish farm at Procklis to the north of Altan Lough.

The key to the starting point (937 255) lies south of the road from Falcarragh to Glenveagh National Park (via Muckish Gap). From the junction in Falcarragh main street, drive for 2km/1.2miles and take the right turn (no signpost) at 943 308 where a road runs south (with open bog on the left). After 2km/1.3 miles it doglegs over a bridge above the old Letterkenny-Burtonport railway. At 4km/2.6miles it bears left (uphill) and continues to the fish farm gates (5km/3.3miles) near Procklis Lough and the hidden Altan Lough.

Park opposite the gates and use the rough track leading to a small farm on the right just north of the bridge over the Tullaghhobegly River. The ascent to Aghla Beg's north-western top begins over slopes of heather and broken bog. Altan Lough soon comes into view, backed by Errigal, with the rump of Muckish to the north. Further up, bear right to keep the high ground around a gully containing the stream issuing from the little corrie holding Lough Nabrackbaddy. The red grouse (*Lagopus lagopus*) can often be raised from this area. Cross another stream before tackling the screes, and then over a fence to the cairn. It opens up your view to the south-east top, 0.8km/0.5miles away and some 12m/40ft higher. Now drop into the dip and ascend the ridge with Lough Aluirg below on the left to reach the small cairn at 580m/1,900ft. Both summits offer superb outlooks, with the boundless Atlantic being the essential element to the west. The latter top overlooks the extensive plantations in the Calabber valley.

A stony descent leads south, levelling out above Lough Feeane, cradled under Aghla More. A simple pull up towards the summit passes an area of wind-eroded peat. The airy summit (584m/1,916ft) is the high noon of the day and an ethereal belvedere for a breather while savouring the view. The south face plunges dramatically to Altan's remote shore, where a sandy beach at the eastern end is overlooked by the gaunt tower of Altan Farm. It was built by John Woodhouse, a Portadown lawyer around the mid nineteenth century. Errigal with its satellite Mackoght, swathed in intimidating screes, commands attention. Beyond lies the granite of the Derryveaghs, culminating with Slieve Snaght, where just to its right a clear day will reveal Benbulbin in distant Sligo.

Now descend the west ridge towards the end of Altan Lough, after a while bearing right to avoid the steeper rocks. Continue down to cross the stream flowing from Lough Feeane, before it enters the lough. Following along the shore, use the stone crossing at the river outlet, where a gated private road joins the tarmac road at Procklis Lough. From here, it is a short distance to the fish farm.

Distance: 9.6km/6 miles. Ascent: 580m/1,900ft. Walking time: 3½ hours.

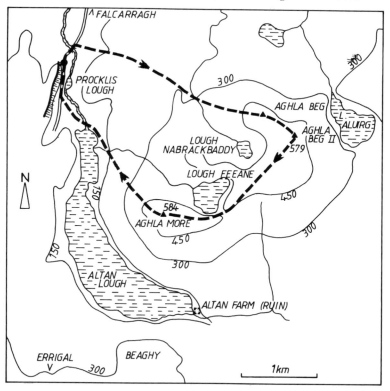

Reference OS Map: Sheets 1 & 2 (1:50,000).

57. HORN HEAD COASTAL WALK

The lofty promontory of Horn Head (Corran Binne, Hook Peak) possesses the highest cliffs on the north Irish coast, and is only rivalled in grandeur by Slievetooey and Slieve League. The neck of sand dunes stretching from Tramore Strand to Horn Head bridge is quite recent, as the promontory was an island in the eighteenth century. Over-cutting of the marram grass in the years 1910–20, combined with storms, led to drifting sands from Tramore virtually sealing off the tidal waters. The former Rinclevan Strand has been transformed into the freshwater New Lake, which is now a wild-fowl sanctuary.

The circular scenic road around the headland misses a great deal of the coastal drama, and short of circumnavigating the cliffs by boat, the hidden extras can only be discovered on foot. The complete round is a long one, but it can be shortened in a variety of ways. Here I describe the western half, starting at Horn Head bridge, which is reached by bearing right off the N56 in Dunfanaghy. There is space for parking off the road beyond Horn Head House entrance gates at 010 376. Return transport can be left, at Coastguard Hill layby, thus saving the 6km/3.5miles road walk back to the bridge. The walk begins by crossing the extensive sand dunes between the New Lake and Anloge Hill. Pass through the stone stile and gate at the north end of the bridge, and walk west to cross a wooden stile at the end of the Horn Head House plantations. The path turns north for a short distance to cross a ditch. From here on, a distinct track leads over the dunes, which are carpeted with wild flowers in early summer. After about 20 minutes you descend to the north end of the pristine Tramore beach, where the whole scene is backed by Muckish and its neighbours a few miles inland.

Continue north on a sheep track over short grass. You cross a pair of small blow-holes known as the Two Pistols with a triangular-shaped entrance cave. Further north, hidden on the surface of the fretted rocks, lies the better known blow-hole of McSwyne's Gun. It is about 190m/200yds north of the small plaque erected in memory of a tragic drowning at the Gun's entrance in 1982. Old guide books claimed that the noise of compressed air forced out of the cavern could be heard up to 32km/20miles away. Now erosion has widened the aperture and the Gun has lost some of its boom. This walk is at its most stimulating when a strong westerly drives the Atlantic combers with frightening force against this intractable coast flinging columns of spray into the air. Then the very ground trembles under the rampaging waves, expelling their energy with a clap of thunder.

The route now leads to Pollaguill Bay following the coast beside a wall over which you descend to the beach — an ideal spot for lunch and a possible bathe, but take heed of the 'Danger — Currents' notice. Continuing out to the cairn on Pollaguill Point, easy ground leads past Croaghadara Hill with Harvey's Rocks off-shore until you arrive at a grandstand view of the superb Marble Arch. The sea has carved this

20m/70ft high arch through the base of Templebreaga Head (*Teampaill na breaga*, Church of Treachery — not named on the OS map). Cross the wall on the right and either ascend over the Head to view the twin tops of Horn Head to the north, or follow the wall which bypasses the summit. Further on, above a deep chasm, *caution is required* where the cliffs rise again at Crockaclogher before dropping over some rock ledges. Lower ground continues over a fence, from where heather slopes leads out to the horns which are split by a gully. The higher western one plunges in a 200m/600ft wall of quartzite to the Atlantic, its numerous ledges providing nesting sites for a variety of sea-birds. As an oceanic belvedere it boasts magnificent views along the north coast from Malin Head to the Bloody Foreland.

The closing stages of the walk take you along the crest of the high cliffs to Traghlisk Point, passing the stump of an old signal tower. From the Point walk south and ascend Coastguard Hill. From the derelict look-out post, use the rough path down to the layby at the end of the scenic road.

Distance: 9.6km/6miles. Ascent: 240m/800ft. Walking time: 3½ hours.

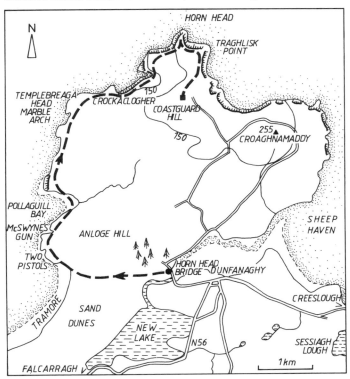

Reference OS Map: Sheet 2 (1:50,000).

58. MUCKISH MOUNTAIN

From most parts of the northwest, Muckish (Muc-ais, Pig's Back: 670m/2,197ft) is one of Donegal's landmarks. Rising from the coastal foothills around Sheep Haven, it is visible from the N56 northwards out of Letterkenny. From then on, its distinctive block form dominates the coast as far as the Bloody Foreland, where its finest elevation shows to advantage near Falcarragh. There are two popular routes offering contrasting terrain to the virtually level summit plateau.

(a) Muckish Gap

The first and easier commences from Muckish Gap (240m/800ft) on the south side, where an unclassified road from Calabber Bridge on R251 crosses the hills to Falcarragh. Starting from the roadside shrine (998 268), an ascent of around 300m/1,000ft up the grassy southeast ridge opens up impressive views through the glacial breach of the Gap. When you reach the plateau rim, walk over the stony wasteland to the large central cairn, almost as high as the official summit. This is at the northern end, across the boulder field and beyond the OS pillar. It is indicated by a stepped plinth surmounted by a simple wooden cross, which has recently (1992) replaced a former more substantial one, erected to commemorate Holy Year in 1950.

The outlook from this northern sentinel is a panoramic feast as it embraces all the intricacies of the coast from Malin Head to the Bloody Foreland, with Tory Island offshore. Diamond-hard visibility will include the top half of Ben More on Mull over 160km/100miles to the north. Southwards, the eye leads over the stark wastes of the plateau to the spine of peaks terminated by Errigal.

The return to Muckish Gap can be made by following the plateau edge westwards where it overlooks the old sand workings, and then by walking south to where the screes fall steeply to the Gap. Retrace your steps down the southeast ridge to the shrine, which is concealed by a knoll as you look from the southern edge.

(b) The 'Miners Track'

This connoisseur's route at the north end has a much more formidable aspect, giving a challenging and pulse-quickening climb, with the added ingredient of a gully descent. It commences at the former sand workings, where fine quality quartzite sand (99% pure silica) used in the manufacture of high quality optical glass was extracted and shipped from nearby Ards pier, until it was officially closed in 1955.

An adequate road leads from the N56, 2km/1.5miles northwest of Creeslough. Turn left (uphill) at a small derelict shop (050 328) and drive for 6km/3.5miles. The route of the Letterkenny and Burtonport railway can be traced on your left. The hard surface ends to the east of Lough Agher.

Walk up the rough track which zigzags for 2km/1.5miles to the old

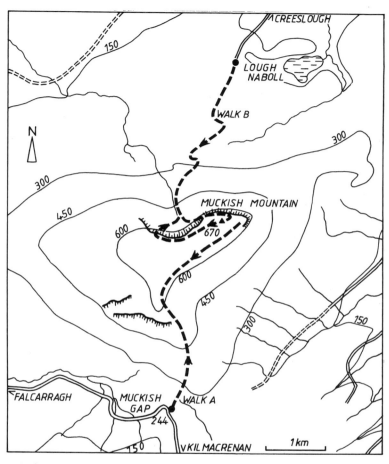

Reference OS Map: Sheet 2 (1:50,000).

loading bays below the conspicuous run of white sand. A rock-fall from the stone-filled gully on the left has engulfed the final section of the track. Cross the stream to the right of the higher loading bay and follow up the broad spur. The climb is a combination of eroded peat and roughly hewn steps. Further up, drop into the left-hand gully and ascend another spur which leads to the base of the rock face. Looking to the right (west) we can see the descent route — a steep but not dangerous gully to the left of the large cave-like opening in the cliff. Continuing upwards, a scant line of posts indicates the path. *This section requires caution.* Above you, vertiginous pinnacles and beetling crags lie below the upper quarry. Further up, the stepped path crosses a small sand-filled gully. The flat floor of the quarry is disfigured with rusting debris. Nowadays, only the plaintive croak of the raven breaks the eerie silence. The inner recesses under the soft friable layers of sandstone provide shelter for a snack.

Leaving the quarry to the left, walk along what was once a stretch of railway and ascend the rough path to the plateau. It is then a level walk over boulders to the OS pillar and the summit plinth. After admiring the view, your return leads northwest above the quarry, where you should descend as far as an outcrop, capped with a flat rock, on the right. It makes a good foreground subject for a 'Miners Track' photo. Two gullies descend from here; the left-hand one ends at the back of the cave (mentioned earlier) and has no through route. Descend the right-hand one and *exercise care with the footwork*. It broadens out into a scree fan, from where you contour across to the stream on the right of the ascent spur. Continue to the top of the white sand run, where a quick scree run finishes at the uppermost loading bay; and hence to the track leading back to the start.

Distance (walk A): 5.6km/3.5miles. Ascent: 420m/1,400ft. Walking time: 2½ hours.

Distance (walk B): 7.2km/4.5miles. Ascent: 450m/1,500ft. Walking time: 3 hours.

59. GLENVEAGH NATIONAL PARK

Prior to 1975, Glenveagh was privately owned and had a great deal in common with the classic Scottish sporting estate. The vast 25,000-acre enclosed deer forest in the mountain heartland of Donegal is based around the breathtakingly beautiful fault valley containing Lough Veagh or Beagh (Beithe, Birch). The Gothic-styled castle built of roughly hewn granite was completed on the bare rocky shore in 1873. Today, it is surrounded by an oasis of trees and gardens, standing as a fairy-tale centrepiece on its promontory above the lough. Above the beach at the head of the lough, the white slide of the Astelleen waterfall completes the romantic highland scene.

In 1981, the late Henry McIlhenny presented the castle and gardens to the nation, and the extended park now includes the peaks of Slieve Snaght and part of Errigal. The only restrictions on hill walkers is that they should not stray from the access roads during the deer-culling season, Mondays to Fridays between 1 September and the end of February.

This walk explores contrasting areas of the park by traversing two summits on the glen's east side, with the return along the lough shore. You have the choice of starting either from the Visitor Centre (highly recommended for its audio-visual show and various displays) or from the main road adjacent to the Administrative/Research buildings. In the summer season (mid April — mid Oct.) you can use the minibus service between the Visitor Centre and the castle. As the hill walk proper starts from the junction of the back avenue from Gartan with the lough shore road (a short distance from the castle avenue) at 028 215, you can arrange to be dropped off there. The current park brochure contains a good coloured 1:50,000 map for this walk.

The initial ascent over rough ground leads to the first top of Altachoastia (225m/737ft) with views over Lough Veagh and the plantation of bottle-green Scots pines, backed by Muckish. Some of the islands were used for illicit distilling in the early nineteenth century. A little west of the summit you look down on the castle and the largest stand of natural woodland in the northwest, flanking the east shore.

Now follow the broad ridge with Lough Nambraddan on your left, backed by Lough Inshagh and its clutch of islets, with part of Lough Gartan in the distance. You will be accompanied by the song of the meadow pipit (*Anthus pratensis*), and the occasional alarm call of the grouse as you move over the impervious granite towards Kinnaveagh (Hill of the Birches: 387m/1,270ft). The gradient steepens over slabs to the cairn, revealing part of Errigal between Dooish (*Dubh-ais*, Black Hill: 654m/2,147ft) and the Poisoned Glen to the northwest. Leahanmore (Big Grey Hill: 445m/1,461ft) to the southwest can be included for a longer day.

At any time on this walk, you should see some of the 500 head of red deer that roam throughout the park. From the cairn, proceed southwest, descending to the top end of Glenlack. A spot near the top of the woods

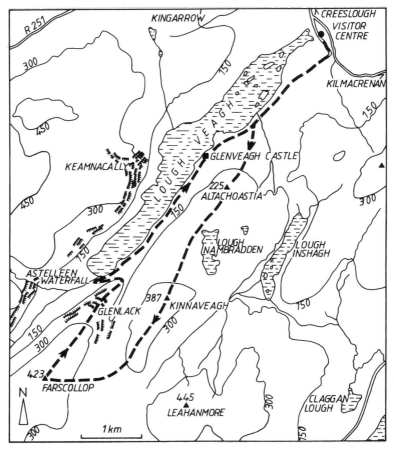

Reference Maps: OS Sheet 6 (1:50,000) or National Park Map (1:50,000).

at the Glenveagh end was the scene of the unsolved murder of James Murray in 1860. He was the agent of John George Adair, the creator of the estate (1857–59). It was this incident that subsequently sparked off an unhappy chapter of tenant evictions in April 1861.

The opposite ridge divides Glenveagh from Glenlack, and a stiff ascent takes you to Farscollop (Outlying Herding Place: 423m/1,388ft) where an indistinct cairn gives a vista southwest to the glen's watershed, flanked by the bulk of Slieve Snaght and the square-headed Moylenaniv. Much of Lough Veagh is hidden from this cairn, and it is not until you drop down the ridge to a rocky spur opposite the Astelleen waterfall that the full glory of the glen is savoured.

The introduced *Rhododendron Ponticum* smothers the western slopes of Farscollop, giving this part of the glen a curiously exotic air. It has been out of control for many years and has had to be ruthlessly cut out of the native woods. Continuing down to the outlying Scots pines, you join the top of the woodland track which angles down to the lough side. It is now a woodland walk of some 3km/2miles along the shore, under a canopy of pine, birch, ash and oak, with tantalising glimpses across the rippling water to the savage crags on the opposite shore.

When you reach the castle, allow time to take in the guided tour of its interior and to discover the astonishing gardens, comprising half a dozen styles. The botanical knowledge started by Mrs Cornelius Adair at the turn of the century has been added to and refined by the artistic sense of the late Henry McIlhenny since the 1940s. Created with a fine feeling for the remote landscape, they are lavishly endowed with exotic plants, together with formal elements. The glen with its high hills and craggy slopes is a natural wind tunnel, and without the vital shelter belt of trees, few of the more delicate species could survive.

Leaving by the castle avenue, you pass through the stately entrance gates surmounted by eagles. Follow the tarred road, fringed with rhododendrons and birch, for 3km/2miles past the gate houses at the outer entrance and hence back to the Visitor Centre.

Distance: 17.6km/11miles. Ascent: 580m/1,900ft. Walking time: 6 hours.

60. MELMORE HEAD COASTAL WALK

Melmore Head (Maol mor, *Great Bald Headland) forms the outer extremity of the Rosguill peninsula* (Ros Ghoill, *Goll's Headland) between Mulroy Bay and Sheep Haven. This walk, which can be done either way round, offers a variety of coastline in a compact area near to Carrickart and Downings and the well-placed Tranarossan youth hostel (*Tra na rossain, *Strand of the Little Promontory).*

Take the R248 from Carrickart towards Downings and bear right (uphill) at the signpost marked Youth Hostel. Join the Atlantic Drive road and continue for approximately 2km/1.5miles, turning right (downhill) at the signpost for Melmore (3km/2.25miles), beyond the viewpoint overlooking Mulroy Bay. Turn left at the bottom of the hill and park at Tranarossan beach car park (119 420).

Walk along the beach to the base of Crocknasleigh Hill (166m/544ft) from where it is a straightforward climb to the highest point on the walk. You now have a view over the whole of your route. To the west the Bloody Foreland looms beyond the back of Horn Head. Eastwards across Mulroy Bay, Knockalla and the north Fanad hills are backed by the Urris group over the concealed Lough Swilly. Southwards, Muckish's slumbering profile presides over Sheep Haven.

Now descend steeply via the shallow depression to the lovely tawny beach of Boyeeghter Bay. At a spot near here known as the Murder Hole, tradition relates that a certain man is said to have thrown his rival in love over the cliff. You can only walk the length of this beach if the tide is well out, as a rocky headland pierced by a cave with a skylight will block further progress. Otherwise descend to the subsidiary top, capped with a ruined look-out post, with a further descent over a wall to the north end of the bay. Due to strong undercurrents, the beach is *dangerous for bathing.*

Easy ground over short grass continues, skirting the head of a narrow creek. The walk can be short-circuited at this point, by crossing the low ground beside Melmore Lough and proceeding hence along the road by the east shore. Northwards you follow along the rocky shore of Claddaghanillian Bay and below the western slopes of Melmore Hill until you reach Melmore Bay. Descend carefully over the rocks to the beach if the tide is out, or else traverse the hillside above the scant line of a wall to the narrow neck of land separating Melmore Bay from Mulroy Bay. Contouring up and around the next hillside leads to the shattered remains of the old signal tower. From here you overlook the rocky finger of Melmore Head. Access across the fretted rocks should only be attempted in calm weather. Horn Head's magnificent cliffs guard the western side of Sheep Haven, with the castellated Tory Island (*Toraigh*, Abounding in Towers) offshore. North-eastwards Dunaff Head is seen beyond Fanad.

The return stages from the tower pass Ravedy Island and its beacon. A few feet of causeway connect it to the mainland. Follow past a small lough and some static caravans to the first of several beaches where you join a tarred road just east of Melmore Lough. You have the choice here of following it back to Tranarossan over the hill to the right of a prominent bungalow, or keeping to the coast leading to the beach at Gortnalughoge Bay. From the beach, cross the green flats to join the road south of the Alpine styled youth hostel under Crocknasleigh. It was built as a summer residence for a Mr Phillimore in 1907, and is reputed (incorrectly) to have been designed by Sir Edward Lutyens. Further along the road towards the right turn for the car park, the cross on your left was erected in 1910 by Mrs Phillimore for use by local worshippers.

Distance: 9.6km/6miles. Ascent: 230m/750ft. Walking time: 3 hours.

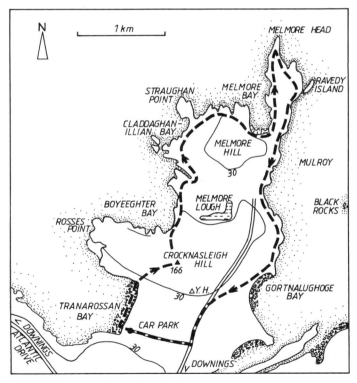

Reference OS Map: Sheet 2 (1:50,000).

61. LOUGH SALT MOUNTAIN

As the highest of a range of hills between Mulroy Bay and Barnes Beg Gap, Lough Salt Mountain commands one of the great viewpoints in the area. It quickly repays the efforts of the walker who embarks on its undemanding ascent. Taking its name (Loch-agus-alt, Lake and Crag) from Donegal's deepest lough cradled under the mountain's western slopes, the triple-topped quartzite summit appears as a blunt coronet on the N56 approach road from Letterkenny.

Bearing right, northwest of Kilmacrenan off the N56, a minor road runs for 7km/4miles over rising ground to the car park/viewpoint on the west side of Lough Salt (122 260).

Walk back along the road to the filter house (the Lough is Letterkenny's water supply), and cross the fence by the stile a little further on. Another stile to the east gives access to the ridge proper, where firm ground ascends for around 240m/800ft, opening up the view over the lough in its glaciated trough. In the 1820s a meteor was recorded as having struck the hillside, and for some years afterwards the scorched heather marked the track of the blazing celestial body where it rolled into the water.

From the first top, follow the dip northwards to the OS pillar on the eroded main summit at 471m/1,546ft. From its relatively isolated position you can observe the pronounced NE–SW geological alignment that characterises much of north Donegal. The pellucid summer light and the constantly shifting cloud patterns enhance the chameleon moods of this northern landscape. It is dominated across Glen Lough by the impressively tabular Muckish and the peaks extending to Errigal, to which the eye is inexorably drawn. North-eastwards, Mulroy Bay and Lough Swilly bite deeply into the land.

Continuing to the stone cairn on the northern summit, the return route is a short descent and then contours towards the small corrie containing Lough Reelan. The final stages descend the steep heather slopes to cross the overflow channel at the northern end of Lough Salt. The grassy hillside between the channel and the road has faint parallel furrows indicating former cultivation.

Return along the road by the lapping waters of this scenic lough for a little over 0.8 km/0.5miles to the viewpoint.

Distance: 5.6km/3.5miles. Ascent: 230m/750ft. Walking time: 2 hours.

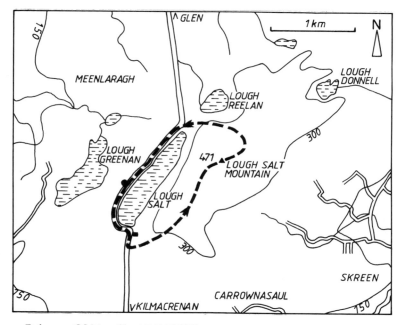

Reference OS Map: Sheet 2 (1:50,000).

62. KNOCKALLA

The Fanad peninsula between Lough Swilly and Mulroy Bay is dominated by Knockalla (Cnoc eala, Hill of the Swan) known locally as the 'Devil's Backbone'. Its northeast end terminates spectacularly at Saldanha Head north of Knockalla Fort built in 1812 to guard the entrance to Lough Swilly against a possible French invasion. The ridge has three tops which are not individually named. It can be walked in either direction with return transport previously left at the layby at Saldanha Head or at the Carrowkeel (Kerrykeel) end.

The walk described here is towards Lough Swilly. The approach road (R246) north from Milford hugs the shore of Mulroy Bay. Passing through Carrowkeel, the R247 to Rathmullan ascends on to the moors for approximately 2km/1.2miles. At the second road fork (for Glencar) there is a convenient layby on the left at 233 330.

Use the rough bohereen leading towards the first of the two south-west tops. When you gain the ridge the whole of its structure is revealed, with the inclined quartzite strata dipping south-eastwards. The well drained ground combined with the rocky outcrops make for an exhilarating traverse, over the 314m/1,032ft top and then on to the main summit at 367m/1,203ft. Westwards you have grand views over Mulroy Bay's complex waters to Lough Salt Mountain, backed by the Derryveagh range.

Now descend towards the twin Knockalla Loughs, nestling beneath the ridge. They can be passed on either side, with the left-hand route crossing the stream between the loughs, where one encounters the only marshy ground. On the right, easy heather slopes over crags take you to another 365m/1,198ft summit. From the cairn one looks over the curving beach of Ballymastocker, forming a golden boundary between the pastoral hinterland underlain by old red sandstone and the blue waters of Lough Swilly. Across its dramatic entrance, the rugged Urris Hills overlook the fortifications on Dunree Head. Southwards, barren moorland stretches towards the Crockanaffrin Hills. In summer you may be lucky to spot (or smell) a herd of feral goats that frequents the ridge.

Leaving the cairn, the route continues over a series of lesser heights passing a pair of lochans on the right and over point 199m/654ft. You then drop steeply to the layby above Ballymastocker beach on the corniche style road between Rathmullan and Portsalon. Below you, Saldanha Head is named after a frigate which foundered in Ballymastocker Bay during a wild storm in 1811 with the loss of 274 hands.

If you have not arranged return transport, a shorter version of the walk leaves the second summit on its south side to join a bohereen leading to Glencar, from where it is 2km/1.2miles back to the starting point.

Distance: 7.2km/4.5miles. Ascent 350m/1,150ft. Walking time: 3 hours.

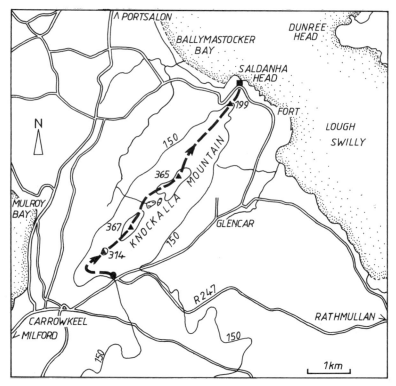

Reference OS Map: Sheet 2 (1:50,000).

63. GLENGAD HEAD COASTAL WALK

The most northerly of these walks takes us to a trackless and remote part of the Inishowen peninsula (Inis Eoghain, Owen's Island). This is an easily graded route along cliffs of quartzite, backed by heather moorland west of Glengad Head. The Atlantic's constant ebb and flow, aided by its artillery of huge breakers during storms, has fashioned the coast between Glengad and Malin Head in a spectacular way not repeated elsewhere in Inishowen with the exception of Dunaff Head.

As this is intended as a one-way walk, return transport should be left, prior to the walk, southeast of Malin Head where an unclassified road leaves the R242 to end steeply at a stony beach on Slievebane Bay beside a ruined church (433 582). Behind the ruin, a small cave known as 'the wee house of Malin' is signposted from the top of the hill. Return to the R242 junction and drive east for about 10km/6miles to the starting point at the scattered settlement of Glentooskert. Turn left at the signpost indicating Malin 14km/9miles (or right if approaching from Culdaff). Take the second turn left and park at a T-junction above a belt of conifers behind some cottages (517 543).

Walk up the road and through a gate, bearing right for the top of the ridge. The craggy top of Croaghglengad is immediately to the south, backed by Slieve Snaght and other hills in central Inishowen. Below, on your right, the hillside plunges to the blunt headland of Glengad (*Gleann na ngad*, Glen of the 'Gads' or Withes) with its look-out post. Breasting the next rise opens up much of the route, with the quartet of skerries known as the Garvan Islands beyond the stack of Stookaruddan. Offshore lies Inishtrahull, composed of Lewisian gneiss, which gives it a geological affinity with the Outer Hebrides. A clear day will reveal Islay and the Paps of Jura some 110km/70miles away on the north-eastern horizon.

A level stretch crosses old peat cuttings and a stream falling over the cliffs. Continue across the eroded peat where a bog road comes in from the left. Keeping strictly and *carefully* to the cliffed edge along the walk is more rewarding as this wild coast unfolds its highlights slowly. On a breezy summer's day the air is filled with wheeling sea birds and the ocean pounds on to inaccessible coves and offshore stacks. Traversing below Crockglacknakinnoge Hill, descend a little and bear right to reach bracken-covered Carrickaveal Point. From here, aim for the small pinnacle about 1.6km/1mile away on the cliffed edge of Crockalough Hill (285m/935ft) across a shallow valley.

This is a fine viewpoint, where Stookaruddan, the Garvan Islands and Malin Head, capped with its old signal tower, make a nice composition. Far below lies a sea stack pierced by an arch. Those with spare energy can ascend to Crockalough (locally called 'the Bens'), the highest point on this coast, to savour much of Inishowen from the radio station and wind charger. Otherwise, descend to the grassy headland close to Stookaruddan, the large offshore stack (73m/239ft) festooned with orange lichen.

The closing stages lead above lesser cliffs and past another arched sea stack. Further on, cross the fence above a hidden beach. Off the coast the Garvan Islands have merged into one. Another fence is crossed beyond some damp ground where several houses appear on the left. Pass above a pair of sandy coves with tide-eroded stacks until a gully on your right leads to a larger storm beach. Accompanied by the kleep-kleep of the oyster-catcher (*Haematopus ostralegus*), continue over its smooth stones to 'the wee house of Malin'.

Distance: 12.8km/8miles. Ascent: 240m/800ft. Walking time: 4 hours.

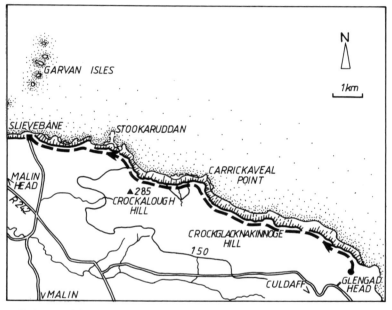

Reference OS Map: Sheet 3 (1:50,000).

64. RAGHTIN MORE AND THE URRIS HILLS

These conspicuous quartzite hills form a serrated back-bone in the northwest of Inishowen and provide a challenging promenade over all the summits. For shorter days, the glacial breach of Mamore Gap (Madhm mor, Great Gap) which is crossed by an unclassified road, can be the starting point in either direction. In this case, return transport should be left at the appropriate end of the ridge.

The described route includes all these summits, beginning with Raghtin More (*Rath Finn Mor*, Finn's Great Rath: 505m/1,657ft) and finishing at Crummie's Bay, east of Dunree Head. Return transport should be left en route at the layby behind the bay at 294 392.

Drive up the Owenerk Valley, passing below Slievekeeragh to the cross-roads west of Clonmany (368 465). Turn left and travel for approximately 0.8km/0.5miles to the bridge at Glen House, where there is a sign marked 'Waterfall'.

Follow the vague track up the delightful Butler's Glen with Raghtin More ahead. It crosses and re-crosses the stream in this miniature valley, mantled with birch and bracken. Soon you will come to a secretive waterfall plunging into a dark pool at its head — a pleasant place for cooling off on a summer's day if doing this walk in reverse. Now climb out of the glen and ascend over tussocky grass and heather towards the steeper ground leading to Raghtin Beg, where northwards over the outlier of Crocklacky you see Glashedy Island, backed by Malin Head with the foreland of Dunaff Head to the west.

The broad ridge leads to Raghtin More's summit with its OS pillar and substantial cairn. South-eastwards, Slieve Snaght dominates central Inishowen. Your route over all the tops now lies towards Lough Swilly (*Suileach*, Abounding in Eyes). The well-drained quartzite ground, characteristic of north Donegal, makes for easy walking to the next top of Crockmain (*Cnoc Meadon*, Middle Hill: 457m/1,500ft), which is followed by a drop, before ascending the knobbly Mamore Hill (421m/1,381ft). From here, one looks across the Mamore Gap to the Urris group.

The sharply inclined rock strata during the descent to the Gap require caution. You may quench your thirst at St Columbkille's Well a short distance down the north side on the left of the road. Back at the summit there is the option of using a rushy track on the south side to bypass the intimidating screes. Leave it after a short distance and climb steeply with the ragged crest of Crockcarragh (*Cruac carrac*, Rough Hill: 381m/1,250ft) ahead. Its pointed outlier to the north can be included. From now on, easy terrain continues over a series of rocky tops and heathery hollows towards the dome of Urris (*Iorrus*, western promontory: 420m/1,379ft). The small valley on the right holds Lough Fad and Cranlough. Urris gives superb views over the remote shore between Lenan Bay (*Lionain*, Filling in [of the sea]) and Lough Swilly's entrance and across to Knockalla on the Fanad peninsula. At one's feet lies Dunree Head (*Dun riogh*, Fort of the King). Military occupation of its fort ceased here in 1990, and a museum is now a tourist attraction.

Continue to the final summit of Crockfadda, where the descent through a mixture of bracken and boulders leads to the beach at Crummie's Bay. Bear left and follow a rough track to join the road near the bridge over the Owenerk River from where it is a short walk to the layby.

Distance: 14.4km/9miles. Ascent: 1,060m/3,500ft. Walking time: 6½ hours.

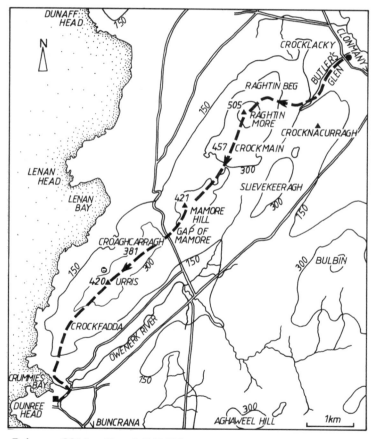

Reference OS Map: Sheet 3 (1:50,000).

65. SLIEVE SNAGHT

Inishowen's reigning summit, Slieve Snaght (Sliabh snechta, *Mountain of the Snows: 615m/2,019ft) rises as a blunt quartzite dome from spacious moorlands in the heartland of the peninsula, 9km/6miles northeast of Buncrana. From the south, the substantial neighbouring hills of Slieve Main* (Sliab Meadon, *Middle Mountain: 475m/1,557ft) and Crocknamaddy* (Cnoc-Maide, *Hill of the Strong Stick: 367m/1,203ft) mask its true elevation. This is only seen to advantage in the north in the vicinity of Carndonagh.*

This walk includes the outlier of Damph (*Dam* [like an] Ox, 422m/ 1,385ft) as well as Slieve Main. Drive north from Buncrana on the main Carndonagh road (R244) and take a right turn for Glentogher. Bear left on to the unclassified road southeast of Damph, passing the scattered houses of Turk. Park about 190m/200yds past the last building on the left (a slate-roofed barn) just before the road drops a little (443 369).

An easy gradient takes you to Damph's broad cairnless summit, with extensive vistas over the conifer plantations towards conical Grinlieve beyond Glentogher. Slieve Main and the bulk of Slieve Snaght are in the opposite direction and frame Raghtin More further northwest.

Now follow a fence downhill into a basin between the hills until it turns right. Cross the fence and stream and ascend to the left towards Slieve Main. After topping a subsidiary shoulder, undulating terrain leads over several bumps where it is difficult to ascertain the highest. Southwards, one looks over the ribbed northern slopes of Crocknamaddy towards Buncrana and Lough Swilly. Northwards, Slieve Snaght's smooth flanks dappled with scree loom close at hand, with Slieve Snaght Beg on the left.

Descending to the col where there are a few peat hags, a climb of 180m/600ft takes you to the stony summit littered with numerous small cairns. Further on, a drystone shelter wall surrounds the OS pillar. A fine day permits a panoramic view over all Inishowen and Lough Foyle, with Lough Swilly backed by the main Donegal Highlands. Far over Inishowen Head, the Hebridean islands of Islay and Jura with its twin Paps can be picked out in exceptional visibility. Looking northwest over the metadolerite outcrops of the King and Queen of the Mintiaghs, the rugged skyline of Urris will hold your gaze.

Slieve Snaght used to be the venue for an annual gathering which took place at the summit spring-well (*Suil-a'-Tobair*). Young people would climb up here, ostensibly to gather heather-berries on the Sunday before 'Gooseberry' fair in Buncrana on 26 July. More often it was a social occasion, with many future weddings resulting. This custom appears to have died out in the early years of the century.

Leaving the cairn, the descent to the east takes you to broken ground, but as there is relatively little bare peat, the going is not arduous. Take a line leading towards the northern end of Damph. Keep the conspicuous rock outcrop on its northwest side to your right. The ground rises for a little and then drops to join the outward route above the road.

Distance: 9.6km/6miles. Ascent: 600m/2,000ft. Walking time: 4 hours.

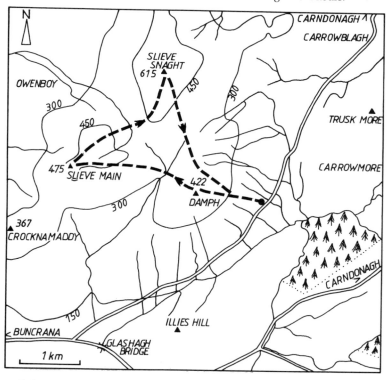

Reference OS Map: Sheet 3 (1:50,000).

66. BINEVENAGH

The basaltic cliffs of Binevenagh (possibly ben-Uaimhneach or Ben-Yevenagh, Terrifying Promontory, but there is no record of this derivation) brooding over the Lough Foyle lowlands impart an atmosphere of grandeur to this corner of Co. Derry. Together with the scarps of Windy Hill to the northeast, the formation is essentially a westward extension of the Antrim plateau. The cliffs form the dramatic centre-piece to a varied walk. Some scrambling experience is essential in order to exit from a gully on to the plateau summit.

The starting point lies off the Leighry Road (704 317) which connects Lower Ballyleighter with the Bishop's Road east of the mountain. Turn right at the school on the A2 between Limavady and Downhill and follow the undulating road along the foot of the extensive plantations, passing a church on your left. Further on, turn right (uphill) for just under 1km/ 0.6miles where there is a clearing marked Binevenagh Forest (new entrance 1993) on the right.

A driveable road to the summit leaves the clearing on the left. Passing by the gate straight ahead, follow the track westwards. There is an expansive view over the Magilligan plain, whose flatness provided the baseline for the Ordnance Survey's first topographical survey of Ireland in 1827. Bearing left at a junction, continue uphill to cross the stile at the forest edge. Traverse upwards across grassy slopes, passing a solitary tree to a blunt pinnacle at the base of the towering cliffs. This is the first of an entourage of similar features, formed it is thought when undercut masses collapsed outwards from the main cliffs when relieved from the supporting weight of the last glaciers. Above you, breeding fulmars (*Fulmarus glacialis*) hover around their roosting places in the basaltic clefts uttering a harsh cracking call.

Beyond the pinnacle, a faint sheep track descends and then rises past a further slumped section. A stream draining the artificial Binevenagh Lake on the plateau above discharges from the deep gully on your left. There is no access out at its top end. Cross the fence beyond the gully and continue around the next cliff bastion. An obvious dry gully appears on your left, just before the track descends into a hollow. Ascend this to its top end. On your left a ¾m scramble over the knobbly basalt with adequate foot- and hand-holds leads to firm grass and rock, where you bear right to emerge on to the plateau rim a short distance above.

As an alternative to continuing the walk to the nearby lake and Croaghan view point a little to its northeast, you can explore the rim of the escarpment to the south which overlooks a pair of conspicuous pinnacles. The cliff-top basalt takes on an almost cyclopean quality in places, while far below the River Roe meanders seawards beside the Bellarena Estate. The whole scene is backed by Lough Foyle and Donegal's Inishowen peninsula.

Binevenagh's actual summit (385m/1,260ft) lies south of the lake, partially surrounded by younger plantations. Returning north to Croaghan view point, use the road which joins the road from the car park which descends eastwards. At the arrowed T-junction take a left turn. On your descent more clear felling has taken place (in 1993) as the track leads you back to the starting point.

Distance: 5km/3.5miles. Ascent: 188m/610ft. Walking time: 2–2½ hours.

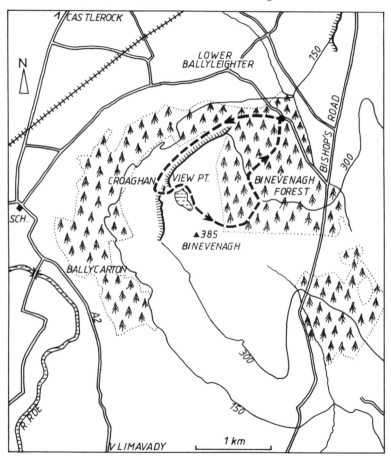

Reference OSNI Map: Sheet 4 (1:50,000).

67. BANAGHER FOREST

Tucked away in the northern foothills of the Sperrin Mountains, this is a circular walk around the Banagher Forest (Beannchar, Place of Pointed Hills) which surrounds the Altnaheglish Reservoir (Alt-na-heghish, Glen of the Church).

Access is by turning right at New Street in Dungiven, and driving south, following the Owenrigh River for 4km/3.1miles to the entrance gate at the end of a No Through Road. Park round the corner beside a wooden hut on the banks of the Owenrigh (671 051).

Passing through the gate, a tarred road crosses the Cushcapel Bridge, near the junction of the Altnaheglish River and Cushcapel Water. It continues past the riverside picnic site, bearing left uphill past a green shed to enter Altnaheglish Glen. Its craggy sides are generously clothed with native tree species such as alder, ash, beech and birch. A bridge carrying a water supply pipeline crosses the Glenedra Water, tumbling through a gorge on the right. A second bridge crosses the Altnaheglish, after which the road takes an easy gradient up the glen. In late spring, a film of bluebells and unfolding ferns carpet the woodland floor, and the air is filled with the chorus of bird song.

Just beyond a cattle grid, there is a good view up the top half of the glen, with the river below. Further up, a stand of conifers masks the Altnaheglish Dam, holding back the reservoir that supplies Derry City. Bear left at a junction to pass a layby which overlooks the dam, with a vista to Glenshane Mountain. The dam was opened in 1935, with a new crest and spillway improvements added in 1987.

Continuing past the dam, a right turn on to a track leads to a gate beside a rain gauge and the all-enveloping conifers. The track swings left, keeping rigidly to the reservoir shore. On your left, a thick belt of cypress trees is followed by stands of pine and Japanese larch. The variety of species makes this forest more interesting and less claustrophobic than the all too ubiquitous Sitka spruce plantations.

At the end of the reservoir, turn right and then right again, and ascend slightly through an avenue of spruce. Soon, the track swings left and then right and then left again at a junction. It then rises past a fire-fighting pool to the highest point on the walk (approximately 360m/1,200ft) on the shoulder of Altnaheglish Hill (377m/1,238 ft). A broad firebreak runs to either side. North-eastwards, the unclassified road between Dungiven and Moneyneany cuts across the landscape.

The track now descends to the west, and distant views are cut off, as you enter the more mature forest at a junction above the Glenedra Valley. Turn right, and follow a level stretch through the trees. After about 2km/1.2miles, you will see the opposite hillside through the larch trees (in winter). A further descent takes you to the bridge over the Glenedra Water. Turn right and follow the river, where you are back into a mossy, deciduous woodland setting again, with the burbling river below. The skyline ahead is topped by a large gravel mound from quarrying activity on Carnanbane Hill.

You keep dropping down, to join the road in Altnaheglish Glen at a point a little above the picnic site on the Owenrigh River, where you are a few minutes from the entrance gates.

Distance: 12.8km/8miles. Ascent: 270m/900ft. Walking time: 4 hours.

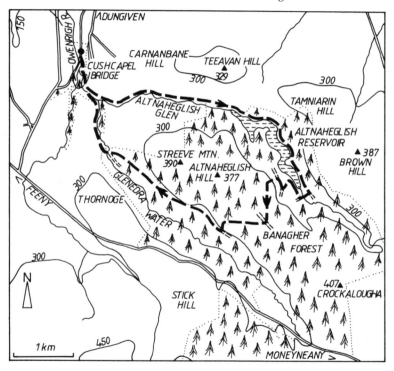

Reference ONSI Maps: Sheets 7 and 8 (1:50,000).

68. THE SPERRINS: SAWEL AND DART

*The rolling country of north Tyrone around Gortin and Glenelly cul-
minates on the county boundary with Derry in the 'high Sperrins'*
(Cnoc speirin, *Pointed hills*). *Rising confidently to over 610m/2,000ft they form
a natural east-west line on the north side of Glenelly. Despite their Irish name, they
display dome-like summits formed from the Dalradian schists. The numerous
supporting flanks are dissected by streams running north and south. Lacking the
resistant quartzites and the geological assertiveness of the neighbouring Donegal
Highlands, these subdued uplands are characterised by flowing curves, and have
a general paucity of corrie lakes and bare rock ridges.*

The entire walk over the Sperrins' five 610m/2,000ft summits gives a full
day's tramp of 29km/18miles, without dropping below the 305m/1,000ft
contour. It starts on Craigagh Hill (off the B40) and finishes at the Butterlope
Glen, north of Plumbridge. This described walk, however, is over the central
section, bounded on the west by Dart Pass (435m/1,426ft), one of the highest
in Ireland and on the east by Sawel or Cloghornagh Pass (337m/1,105ft).
The route takes you over the principal summit of Sawel (*Sabhal*, Barn: 683m/
2,240ft) and Dart (*Darta*, Mountain of the Yearling Heifers: 622m/2,040ft).

Drive up the verdant Glenelly valley, east of Plumbridge on the
Draperstown road (B47). The lower Sperrins enclose the south side, broken
by the glacial spillway of Barnes Gap. Beyond Cranagh, the Sperrin Heritage
Centre gives a visitor a good introduction to the region which has an Area
of Outstanding Natural Beauty status. Continue to Sperrin hamlet (Mount
Hamilton) and turn left for Park (10km/6.5miles). The road climbs steadily
to the head of the Pass, where you can park at a layby beyond a cattle grid.

Ascend the east flank of Sawel, where from the first rise above some
rocks, you view the northern side of the Pass, backed by Barnes Top. Follow
the fence on your left over a mixture of grass and heather with some broken
peat for around 305m/1,000ft, until the fence bears left. Keeping straight
ahead, you emerge on to the spacious summit at the OS pillar — a place to
relax and brew-up after the last hour's exertions.

Sawel's central position ensures a vast panorama on a good day, when
you can see from the Mournes and the Antrim hills in the east to the whole
miscellany of the Donegal Highlands in the west, with the Fermanagh/
Cavan uplands in the south. Northwards is the Glenshane Pass and the
scarps of Donalds Hill and Binevenagh, forming a westward extension of
the Antrim plateau country, overlooking the Foyle lowlands, backed by
the Inishowen Hills.

Crossing the stile over the fence, you descend to lower ground over
eroded peat towards Dart, which appears satisfyingly close. A more interesting approach to its summit is by traversing right to explore the knuckles
of rock enlivening the north side. This is the one and only substantial
outcrop on the whole Sperrin range, and may have been formed by glacial
plucking. From the cairn, the great whaleback of Mullaghclogha, the

second highest in the Sperrins, dominates the west, across Dart Pass. The road from Cranagh can be seen, snaking up above an isolated farm.

Leaving the summit, return to the broad col between Dart and Sawel and traverse the southern slopes of the latter. Further on, a grassy ravine is crossed, where afterwards you continue to contour slightly downhill to join the fence which leads down to Sawel Pass.

Distance: 8km/5miles. Ascent: 450m/1,500ft. Walking time: 2½–3 hours.

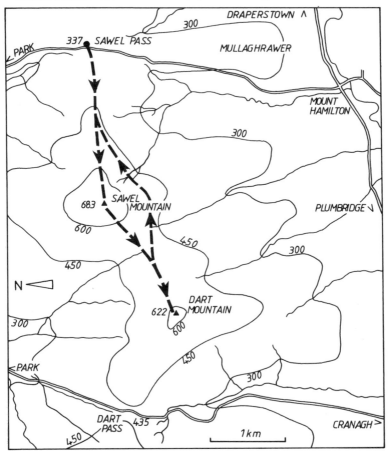

Reference OSNI Map: Sheet 13 (1:50,000).

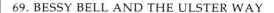
Assuming an almost mountainy elevation from the A5 road between Strabane and Newtownstewart, Bessy Bell (420m/1,378ft) presides over the mature landscapes of the Strule and Mourne River valleys in west Tyrone. Heavily mantled on its western side by the conifer plantations of the Baronscourt Estate, a gentle south-western outlier terminates at Manus Hill (258m/848ft). Choosing a haze-free day with the prospects of good visibility, this relatively isolated hill yields wonderful views, out of all proportion to its modest height, and is in some ways superior to the high Sperrins.

Start almost at the road junction (near Baronscourt Garden Centre entrance) on the B84 with the unclassified road to Mountjoy which runs between Manus Hill and Bessy Bell. The approach road from Omagh is via the A5 and Mountjoy, that from Newtownstewart is via the B84.

Use the green track at 367 822 up through Sadler's Wood, which has a cleared area on your left. Felling and replanting is continuous on this large commercially run estate, which has plans for increased sporting and recreational facilities. From the off-set crossroads at the top of the wood, follow the Ulster Way sign uphill. The track clears the trees at around 350m/1,150ft and continues to the British Telecom aerial on the summit.

Nearby is an ancient stone tomb known as Donald Gorm's Cairn, which was excavated in 1900 and found to contain bones and ashes. A little to the south, a Holy Well called Toberneill, marked by a short post, is credited with making your wishes come true by dropping three stones into it. An immense spread of country can be seen all around. As this is the most inland summit in this guide, the familiar Atlantic is absent. Tyrone's county town, Omagh, nestles at the upper end of the Strule valley to the southeast. Bessy Bell's diminutive 'sister', Mary Gray (252m/ 828ft), across the valley is the tail end of a line of low hills including the evocative sounding Beauty Hill and Robbers Table, that run towards the Gortin Gap. Bessy Bell and Mary Gray were formerly named Slieve Trim (Hill of the Elders) and Carnaveagh (Brae of the Birches) respectively. They were renamed by Scottish settlers who came to Newtownstewart, in memory of two Perthshire cousins who died of the plague in 1666. Another tradition relates that Bessy Bell derives its name from an idol called Bell, whose religious rites, performed on the summit during pagan times, were called Baase, hence Baase Bell meant the ceremonies of Bell, later becoming corrupted to Bessy Bell.

While Newtownstewart is concealed by the northern spur, the jostling line of the Sperrins rise above the Glenelly valley. Westwards, you look over Baronscourt, the home of the Duke and Duchess of Abercorn. Its centre-piece is the fine Georgian mansion built in 1741 close to three artificial lakes and surrounded by gardens and parkland. Away in the far northwest, Muckish and the pyramidal Errigal pierce the skyline. You can also identify every other top, from Slieve Snaght in Inishowen right round to the sharp edge of Benwhiskin in distant Sligo. Southwards, over the Drumquin hills, the Cuilcagh ridge dominates the horizon.

From the summit, there are alternative descents to the road northeast of Manus Hill, either by way of the forest cross roads and turning left, following the Ulster Way, or a more arduous tramp above the plantations, through deepish heather. The latter route leads down past ten wind generators. Continue past a smaller plantation and then across a field to the road. Follow the Ulster Way sign a little way up the road to the left, to enter Manus Wood. The exemplary signposting at each track junction leads you through to the B84. You may be lucky, as I was, to see one or two of the 500 head of Sika deer that roam throughout the Estate. The Ulster Way leaves the B84 to the left at a stone cottage, but you keep straight on for 1.6km/ 1mile, passing the Garden Centre entrance on the left, back to the start.

Distance: 8.8km/5.5miles. Ascent: 300m/1,000ft. Walking time: 3 hours.

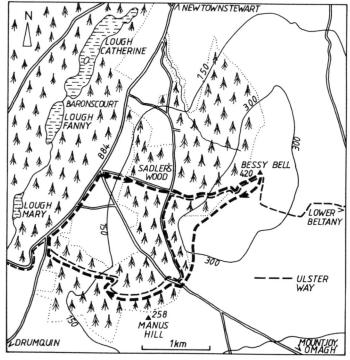

Reference OSNI Map: Sheet 12 (1:50,000).

BIBLIOGRAPHY

General

Charlesworth, J.K., *The Geology of Ireland: An Introduction*, London 1966.

Dillon, P., *The Mountains of Ireland*, Milnthorpe 1992.

Evans, E.E., *The Personality of Ireland*, Cambridge 1973.

Fewer, M., *The Way-marked Trails of Ireland*, Dublin 1996.

Harbison, P. (ed.), *The Shell Guide to Ireland*, Dublin 1989.

Hart, H.L., *Climbing in the British Isles, Ireland*, reprint Holyhead 1981.

Holland, C.H. (ed.), *A Geology of Ireland*, Edinburgh 1981.

Joyce, P.W., *Irish Names of Places*, vols 1, 2, 3, London 1973.

Lynam, J. (ed.), *Best Irish Walks*, Dublin 1997.

Lynam, J., *Irish Peaks*, London 1982.

Mitchell, F., *The Way that I Followed*, Dublin 1990.

Moriarty, C., *A Guide to Irish Birds*, Cork 1967.

Pochin Mould, D.D.C., *The Mountains of Ireland*, Dublin 1976.

Praeger, R.L., *The Botanist in Ireland*, Dublin 1934.

Praeger, R.L., *The Way that I Went*, Dublin 1969.

Whittow, J.B., *Geology and Scenery in Ireland*, Harmondsworth 1974.

West

Archer, J.B. and Ryan, P.D., *The Caledonides of Western Ireland*, Dublin 1983.

Cunningham, G., *Burren Journey West*, Limerick 1978.

Herman, D., *Hill Walkers Connemara and Mayo*, Dublin 1996.

Lynam, J., May, J. and Robinson, T.D., *The Mountains of Connemara — A Hill-walker's Guide*, Roundstone 1988.

O'Connell, J.W. and Korff, A. (ed.), *The Book of the Burren*, Kinvara 1991.

Robinson, T.D., *Burren* (Map), Roundstone 1977.

Robinson, T.D., *Connemara, Introduction, Gazetteer and Map*, Roundstone 1990.

Webb, D.A. and Scanell, M.J.P., *Flora of Connemara and the Burren*, Cambridge 1983.

Whilde, A., *Birds of Galway and Mayo*, Dublin 1977.

Whilde, A., *Birds of Galway*, Galway 1990.

Whilde, A., *The Cliffs of Moher*, Belfast 1987.

Whilde, A., *The Natural History of Connemara*, London 1994.

North

Hamill, J., *North Ulster Walks Guide*, Belfast 1987.

Herman, D., *Hill Walkers Donegal*, Dublin 1995.

Warner, A., *Walking the Ulster Way*, Belfast 1989.

GLOSSARY

Glossary of the more common Irish words used in Place Names

Abha, abhainn (ow, owen)   river
Achadh (agha, augh)   field
Ail or *Faill*   cliff
Alt   height or side of glen
Ard   height, promontory
Ath ford

Baile (bally)   town, townland
Bán (bawn, baun)   white
Barr   top
Beag (beg)   small
Bealach (ballagh)   pass
Beann (ben)   peak or pointed mountain
Bearna (barna)   gap
Bignian   little peak
Bó   cow
Bóthar (boher)   road
Bothairin (bohereen)   small (unsurfaced) road
Breac (brack)   speckled
Brí (bree, bray)   hill
Buaile (booley)   summer dairy pasture
Buí   yellow
Bun   foot of anything, river mouth

Carn   pile of stones
Carraig (carrick)   a rock
Cathair (caher)   stone fort
Ceann (ken)   head, headland
Ceathramhadh (carrow)   quarter of land
Ceapach   plot of tillage ground
Cill   cell, church
Clár   plain, board
Cloch   stone
Clochóg   stepping stones
Cluain (cloon)   meadow
Cnoc (knock, crock)   hill
Coill (kyle, kill)   wood
Coire   cauldron, corrie
Cor   rounded hill
Corrán (carraun)   sickle, serrated mountain
Cruach, cruachan   steep hill (rick)

Cúm (coum)   hollow, corrie
Dearg   red
Doire (derry)   oakgrove
Druim   ridge
Dubh (duff, doo)   black
Dún   fort, castle

Eas (ass)   waterfall
Eisc (esk)   steep, rocky gully

Fionn (fin)   white, clear
Fraoch (freagh)   heath, heather

Gabhar (gower)   goat
Gaoith (gwee)   wind
Glas   green
Glais   streamlet
Gleann (glen)   valley
Gort   tilled field

Inbhear (inver)   river mouth
Inis   island

Lágh (law)   hill
Leac   flagstone
Leaca, leacan (lackan)   side of a hill
Leacht   huge heap of stones
Learg   side of a hill
Leitir (letter)   wet hillside
Liath (lea)   grey
Loch (lough)   lake or sea inlet
Lug, lag   hollow

Machaire (maghera)   plain
Mael, maol (mweel)   bald, bare hill
Maigh   plain
Mám, madhm (maum)   pass
Más   long, low hill
Mór (more)   big
Muing   long-grassed expanse
Mullach   summit

Oilean   island

Poll   hole, pond

Riabhach   grey
Rinn   headland
Rua, ruadh   red

Scairbh (scarriff) shallow ford
Scealp rocky cleft
Sceilig (skellig) rock
Sceir (sker, pl. skerry) rock, reef (Norse)
Sean old
Sescenn (seskin) marsh
Sidh (shee) fairy, fairy hill
Sliabh (slieve) mountain
Slidhe (slee) road, track
Spinc pointed pinnacle
Srón nose, noselike mountain feature
Sruth, sruthair, sruthán stream
Stuaic (stook) pointed pinnacle
Suí, suidhe (see) seat

Taobh, taebh (tave) side, hillside
Teampull church
Tír (teer) land, territory
Teach house
Tobar well
Tor tower-like rock
Torc wild boar
Tulach little hill